RIDE

THE

TORNADO

*Continuously Improve Your Marketing
Strategy in the Midst of Rapid Change*

TOBIN LEHMAN

To Jennifer. My Love.

Waxwing Insights
125 S. Carroll Street Ste 104
Frederick, MD 21701

ISBN: 978-1-7360610-0-8 (paperback)
ISBN: 978-1-7360610-2-2 (hardcover)
ISBN: 978-1-7360610-1-5 (ebook)

Ordering Information:
Special discounts are available on quantity purchases by corporations, associations, and others. For details, contact info@newnorth.com

TABLE
OF CONTENTS

FOREWORD

My car lurches toward the median, autumn leaves swishing across the hood as I drive home on a cold and gusty October night. In the midst of the blustering noise, an alert dings at the top of my phone, drawing my attention to a tornado warning that has been issued for our area. High winds, debris and uncertainty are the key ingredients to watch for.

Modern marketing is like driving through a tornado. We're all driving through a whirlwind development of new media, marketing channels and ways to connect with customers. New information comes in and spins out with the same chaotic bluster as these winds pushing across the windshield of my car—and with seemingly the same force, tenacity and potential for damage.

A tornado is a great visual depiction of the decision-making questions that leaders and CEOs like you and I answer every day:

* *How do I navigate the constantly changing and uncertain world of digital lead generation for my business?*

* *How do I know how to wisely invest our money for the best return?*

* *What is the best use of my salesperson's time?*

* *And are digital media and online marketing really the panaceas we all dream of?*

These are hard questions, especially for growing businesses like yours. But for a minute, imagine that you own a digital marketing agency that is expected to live on the bleeding edge of all of this transformation while offering rapidly developing and highly effective services to hundreds of businesses like yours. It can be nerve-wracking.

My company and I have been doing this for the past two decades. My personal history in the marketing field starts before Facebook, before Google—before any of the digital media marketing platforms we have now even existed.

I belong to the small section of a generation that entered the workforce right at the beginning of this huge digital transformation. And I have been able to ride that wave to a place of leadership in this field. I say this not to toot my own horn, but to tell you in all humility: This is difficult work. Staying in front of all the change that happens so rapidly is the hardest part of running a business, period. If you multiply the difficulty of that times the dozens of active engagements we have right at this moment, it becomes a major feat, akin to the tricks those plate spinners pull off at the circus.

Thankfully, if you aren't a digital marketer, your industry's rate of change may be slower than ours. But the methodology and thinking behind our approach will certainly help you to generate success amid the changes in your own industry—and, ultimately, clear the path you need for continued success in the years to come.

I'll share with you both a framework for making decisions in tornadoes and practical tips for coming out a little wiser, a little healthier and a little bit more profitable in the end. So, let's begin.

INTRODUCTION

YOUR FIELD GUIDE

My hope in writing this book is that it will become a field guide of sorts to your marketing process. The book is broken up into three sections. The format will allow you to read the entire volume, then return as needed to specific parts for guidance and insight as you explore the entirety of the decision-making cycle and make it your own.

In the first section, we will discuss the case for this type of approach by exploring the speed of change in our working world. This includes an honest assessment of both our internal working environments and the rapid pace of external change that dominates our lives. We'll then shift into how this approach fights (and successfully wins) against the challenges of change as we make a case for rapid thinking. This section will set our perspective as we enter into the RTX Framework itself. The RTX Framework stands for Rapid Thinking & eXecution, a three-phased approach that will radically reshape your approach to marketing.

In the second section, we'll explore the mindset and leadership roles that you will need to take to successfully enact the RTX Framework in your organization. This will include a comprehensive overview of each section of the cycle, with details around how you should approach the framework mentally and how you can lead implementation with your team. This will allow you to get your bearings before you dive into practice.

Lastly, we'll explore implementation and case studies to help you see the cycle in action. The framework is a blend of elbow-grease theory and hard-won tactics—and sometimes it helps to see the ideas put into a real-world context to build understanding. This section will show you how to put the ideas into practice in your company today, with sample agendas, FAQs and guidance on communication with your team. Additionally, we'll explore some of the challenges that come up throughout the cycle to help you when things go awry and you don't get the results you'd expect.

SECTION 1:

A CASE FOR RAPID THINKING

We started 2020 in a strong economic climate, with a stock market at near record highs, low interest rates and wide-open opportunity for many businesses. Less than a month into the year, the world lurched off its axis.

That's the high-level view, anyway. But in real life, inside the walls and offices of businesses like yours, the frantic pace of change is causing unprecedented turmoil. Workers are busier than ever before. Deadlines, production and output are expected at insane, never-before-seen paces. And, in most industries, the competition in the marketplace has become more aggressive, forcing lower profit margins. Companies rise and fall faster than ever before and we are left wondering: What is the catalyst behind this tattered state?

CHA

N G E

This is not yesteryear's "who moved my cheese?" type of change—but rather market fluctuations, process improvements and technology changes that are happening at a pace never before seen in our culture. You might not know what to call it, but you feel it in your gut. And you're feeling the implications in all areas of your life. We're busier than ever before.

Let's take a look at some of the data around the frenetic pace in our lives to see what makes up this "tornado" of change.

FEELING THE SPEED OF CHANGE
New Means Unknown

Generally, the faster change happens, the less confident we are in our ability to make decisions. Change simply makes it harder to make decisions—or, rather, the uncertainty that can accompany change makes it harder to make decisions. (Not all change brings great levels of uncertainty, but in this book, we'll be dealing with the types of change that do. This is the kind of change that causes our worst or best leadership tendencies to surface.)

Recent research has demonstrated that increased levels of uncertainty during organizational changes in the workplace can induce major physiological strain, leading to challenges in communication structures and decreased job satisfaction.

Yet if you've spent any time in the business world, you don't need science to quantify what you already know. People react to uncertainty with a wide range of responses. Some people shut down and make no decisions; some people make unwise decisions quickly. Some people may get emotional, while others will simply lose their minds in anger or blame. All of these reactions are proof positive of the fact that facing the unknown is hard. We can ignore the unknown easily enough, but facing it to make decisions in the blustering gusts of uncertain change can leave even the most fearless leaders grasping for a handrail.

If change intimidates you, you're not alone.

TECHNOLOGY ADOPTION IN US HOUSEHOLDS, 1930 TO 2019

Technology adoption rates, measured as the percentage of households in the United States using a particular technology.

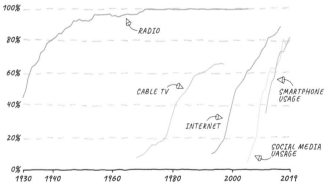

Source: Comin and Hobijin (2004) and others
Note: See the sources tab for definitions of household adoption, or adoption rates, by technology type.

The reality is that in the scope of digital marketing, the pace of change has been increasing rapidly. The data below, depicting the release dates of platforms and technologies in the marketing space over the last few decades, bears this out.

This is the theory of Moore's Law beautifully played out in our real-world context. From the chart above, you can clearly see how the rate of channel and technology introduction into the marketing space has increased at a staggering rate. Just 30 years ago, the only technology a marketing and sales team needed to succeed in business was a telephone. To say things have changed is an understatement. This grand shift has given rise to a sea of ever-more-advanced technologies, and the rate of technological development is not slowing down.

But what does this mean for you? It means that new is not going to slow down anytime soon. To survive, you must develop a way to see new things as opportunities, in spite of the uncertainty they bring. You must learn to review and capture the value of these technologies as quickly as possible.

Yes, We Can Measure Everything

What an amazing world we have in the 21st century. We have more data on every aspect of human life

[1](https://go.forrester.com/blogs/hadoop-is-datas-darling-for-a-reason/)

and interaction than we've ever had before. In fact, we collect data faster than we can analyze, understand and act on it; a recent study found that 65% of companies are collecting data faster than they can use it.[1] We are becoming literally buried in data. The question is no longer, "can we get data on that?" but rather, "what do we do with it?"

The rate of data collection can either create a market advantage for your company or leave your organization handicapped. What would it mean to create 5%–15% more margin simply by collecting and analyzing the data that's generated by your existing systems and processes? As the guru Peter Drucker famously said, "What gets measured improves." The careful act of measuring your business can have a huge impact on your success.

But there are challenges.

First of all, unless you're in a major corporation, most of the "Big Data Analytics" tools are probably out of your reach for the foreseeable future, both because they require technical skill to use and because they're prohibitively expensive. So while you might have some idea of the range of data that exists within your organization, you're likely limited in your ability to determine what data you should focus on to generate insight and solve big problems.

[2](IBM, https://techjury.net/stats-about/big-data-statistics/#gref)

Following that train of thought: Even if you know *what* data you're looking for, you probably don't have a way to capture it all. Real-time data acquisition and processing tools can have fascinating applications for your business, but to implement them at scale takes considerable effort and capital.

Consider this: 90% of all the data in the world has been created in the past two years.[2]

That number is increasing at an exponential rate. We're heading toward numbers far bigger than we could ever envision.

And this data does not stop when you leave the office. When you head home, your personal life is inundated with the same onslaught of information and data about anything and everything. As a society, we are watching more TV than ever. We spend hours each day on social media and our phones. We are in constant information overload, and we do it to ourselves. We are constantly creating data and trying to understand it, but we've whipped it up into a wave that is too tall and too deep to surf.

Does any of this surprise you? Yet let's consider the elephant in the room—and no, it's not the data. If the *amount* of data was so important to the success of any given business, how did the Rockefellers, Fords and Carnegies create such empires? Simple. They didn't have a huge *amount* of data. They had the *right* data.

The data you collect will only be as valuable as the insight and actions you generate from it.

Even in this age of unprecedented prosperity in business (which is largely a result of data-driven decision-making), success is still determined not by how much you measure, but by what you measure. It's always been this way—and it will continue to be. We've simply become distracted from that reality by the sheer volume of data that's available. In our confusion, we've accelerated our investments in data tools that provide plenty of knowledge but very little insight.

Why Are We So Busy?

Even if you were able to slow the rapid influx of information that's piling up on your desk and lighting up your phone, there's another obstacle to your sanity, and it's sitting in your chair.

It's you. You're too busy.

This is becoming an epidemic in the U.S. It's not just waxing poetic about the good old days before technology to say that our busyness is causing us issues. Look at these stats on the next page from the Harvard School of Public Health.

The figures from this study show just how nuts things are getting. We're getting sick more often, and our illnesses are directly tied to stress, busyness and the lack of sound priorities in our lives. We're juggling so much that we're dropping our health. We've all heard the term "working ourselves to death." What was once a cliché is becoming a fact.

This is a serious epidemic in our culture, but the point of this book is not to solve this problem. It's important to implant this correlation in your mind, so that you can be shaken awake to the fact that your busyness isn't a badge of honor any more than a heart pacemaker would be a trophy.

One of the side effects of increased busyness is a decreased ability to focus. We're doing so much that we can't stop to think about what we're doing, and this creates disastrous outcomes in our business and personal lives. We're constantly distracted. From social media, to task switching, to email, the trappings of modern society have us constantly thinking about something else so that we never give any one thing the focus it truly needs.

When we are too busy to focus, we cannot make good decisions. Our brains can't get into a deep-thinking mode; they simply try to spin off an answer that will make the problem go away. We don't take the time to determine whether our problems of the moment are problems worth solving, and we rarely

MOST STRESSFULL EVENTS AND EXPERIENCES IN THE PAST YEAR

Illness and disease	27%
Death of a loved one	16%
Problems with work	13%
Life changes and transitions	9%
Family events and issues	9%
Problems with personal relationships	6%

Source: NPR, Robert Wood Johnson Foundation, and Harvard School of Public Health

MOST COMMON CONTRIBUTORS TO STRESS AMONG AMERICANS WITH GREAT DEAL OF STRESS

Too many responsibilities overall	54%
Problems with finances	53%
Work problems (among employed)	53%
Health problems	38%
Health problems for people in immediate family	37%
Problems with family members	32%
Being unhappy with the way you look	28%

Source: NPR, Robert Wood Johnson Foundation, and Harvard School of Public Health

TOP RESPONSES TO STRESS AMONG AMERICANS WITH GREAT DEAL OF STRESS

Sleeping less	70%
Eating less	44%
Exercising less	43%
Attending religious services or praying more	41%
Sleeping more	41%
Less sex	40%

Source: NPR, Robert Wood Johnson Foundation, and Harvard School of Public Health

arrive at truly helpful answers. We make decisions in haste, without really weighing the factors involved. This approach inevitably wastes time and money. It will certainly leave you regretting your marketing and advertising spends.

It just feels like it's all too much to handle.

Pace of Business Change

So, our access to new technologies is increasing every day. We have more and more data available to us by the minute. And we lead busier lives than humans ever have before in history. What does all of this mean for the nation and for business?

It means that business are changing at paces never before seen. And it means that we are less equipped to handle change.

The chart below shows innovation rates by industry sector in the U.S. The rate of change varies across industries but, taken together, the numbers show one clear and overarching reality: The business world is innovating at a faster rate than any human or organization has ever experienced in the past. Some industries are innovating at rates of 2%–4%. Some are changing at rates that seem more modest—but even for these industries, rates are often two times what they were in previous decades.

When industries aren't changing, big tech and venture capital firms break in and cause disruption to capitalize on convention and outdated business models. Look at what happened to the taxi space with Uber, or to the real estate market with sites like Zillow. The reality is that you can either push forward with change or get blown away by the squall of innovation and money looking for an industry that is not keeping up with the times.

Yet what's most concerning about this reality is that most small-business leaders lack a framework for navigating change.

R&D SPENDING, US$ BILLIONS

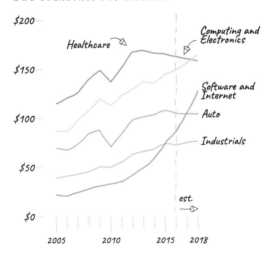

Source: Bloomberg data, Capital IQ data, Strategy & analysis

The leadership lessons and management mantras of the past just don't work in today's fast-paced arenas of change. There's no rule book on using information to your advantage to get ahead. You must learn how to plan for and react to changes. And, most important, you must learn to drive forward, riding the tornado with confidence.

The Speed of Change is Wicked

If you haven't felt it before, you probably do now. You're like the frog in the boiling water. Change will surely disrupt your business, and it might even kill you.

The pace of change is not going to slow down. You must find ways to adapt and take advantage of these innovations—before some other company does and dominates your market. You owe it to your employees, you owe it to your shareholders and you owe it to yourself to learn to ride the pace of change. The framework in this book will help you to navigate it carefully and successfully to keep your business moving forward.

Yet as we move forward, let's not forget where we are coming from—and what is coming for us!

A CASE FOR RAPID THINKING & EXECUTION

Death to the Long-Term Plan

In this era of rapid change, we must kill the common approach to long-term planning. Know that this doesn't mean that you should live or work day to day without ever paying mind to the future—that would be disastrous. Rather, you need to set aside the rigid mentality of long-term planning and replace it with a model that is better equipped to handle the pace of change that we all face.

You've no doubt heard stories of companies contracting software or hardware installations over long-term periods of 18 or 24 months, only to finally launch an obsolete software that fails instantly. I'm sure you've seen this phenomenon in other places, too—maybe even in your own business. It's typically caused by two misconceptions that are common in traditional long-term plans: first, an underestimation of the change that will happen in the external environment, and second, an underestimation of the internal barriers that will hinder project completion. Taken together, these two misconceptions lead to faulty plans. Traditional long-term plans don't accurately account

The natural response to this, then, is to

think in shorter planning cycles.

for change and uncertainty, and so they're rarely realistic.

There are certain fields where external change happens more slowly. In the manufacturing industry, for example, material selections and manufacturing methods may not have changed dramatically in the last five or 10 years, depending on the subsector that you're in. In the technology industry, though, nothing is the same today as it was three years ago. The rate of change in your external environment should impact your method of planning. Any plan you create must take into account where things will be when execution finally happens.

Another reason long-term plans are difficult is that you probably don't create accurate project projections. There's simply too much uncertainty. Even the best, most experienced project managers in any industry know from the Pareto Principle that a project plan is only 80% accurate at best. The reason is actually quite simple: Talented project managers recognize that they can't account for everything. A level of uncertainty exists in any project, and the longer the project rolls on, the higher that level creeps. In other words, the traditional long-term plan makes accurately predicting outcomes more difficult by its very nature. You can go so far as to create fantastic,

So, "yes" to planning, "no" to overplanning and committing to long-term models that will become obsolete before projects are complete.

data-driven models that express how project length impacts measures of uncertainty (and many Ph.D. students do), but what's the point? If you've managed any project, you've experienced this reality firsthand.

When you realize that external change is bearing down on your organization and that even internally there are uncertainties you can't fully predict, you begin to see the world for what it really is.

The natural response to this, then, is to think in shorter planning cycles.

That means building plans that adjust to the environment—plans that work with and flex to changing factors instead of staying static. Focused, short-term plans will help you meet your goals more effectively than idealized, long-term plans that are too rigid.

To avoid planning errors, you must couple a strong long-term vision with short-term plans in iterative cycles to meet your goals. You should plan projects in shorter, detailed cycles, then reevaluate progress and success when a cycle is complete. Taking this approach will allow you to move far more efficiently toward your goal than if you carried out rote execution of an idealized plan over 24 months.

A great example of an ineffective long-term planning approach in the workplace is the formalized business plan. If you've taken any business classes in higher education, you've likely encountered the exercise of creating a business plan. These lengthy and robust documents are great tools to capture thinking and explain your business concepts to investors or college professors. But they're being used less and less in the business world, largely due to many of the factors we've covered here. While research shows that the act of planning itself is still tied to overall company performance, it also shows that success is less tied to any type of written document, such as a business plan, and more dependent simply on having a planning process.

So, "yes" to planning, "no" to overplanning and committing to long-term models that will become obsolete before projects are complete.

To make the most of your efforts, you need to create methods of planning and executing that account for the change and uncertainty that you operate in. Using shorter action cycles and consistently realigning your plans achieves this more effectively.

Call It Agile, Call It Lean, Call It Smart

If you are familiar at all with these arguments for short-term planning, you are either just smart or you've crossed paths with Agile, Lean or some variation thereof. If you aren't familiar with these methodologies, it's time for a short primer on Agile.

First, don't get confused by all the jargon. If you've heard of Agile, that fact is of little benefit. Actually, it's almost better if this is your first exposure to the concept. The preconceived notions that accompany Agile are some of its biggest problems. To make matters worse, there are lower layers of jargon, too; you have Agile development, Agile process meetings, scrum, Kanban and about 20 other different catchphrases that all sound like menu items at Panera. In general, the blogosphere and countless corporate consultants have highjacked Agile terminology and applied it to everything as a wonderful fix-it-all for any business process. And while Agile thinking can improve just about any process, it's not a cure-all.

Agile is not a cure-all because Agile is not a solution in itself.

You don't buy Agile by the pound, you don't flip a switch to become Agile and you surely don't learn Agile in a seminar. With all due respect to the Agile and Lean consultants out there (many of whom, in fact, are probably nodding in agreement with these points), Agile is much more a philosophical approach to work than it is a simple solution.

To be Agile is to attain a way of being and thinking, not just to practice a labeled set of tools and tricks (and it's the promise of quick-and-easy tricks that draw so much attention to Agile). In other words,

Agile is an approach to solving a problem, not a pre-defined process in itself.

Still, what is Agile? There are many different responses to this question, but the most appropriate definition of the term is this: To be Agile is to have a mental framework for problem solving that allows for open exploration, rapid execution and quick feedback toward a specific goal.

Notice two things. First, Agile is a mental framework. It's not a board you can hang on the wall, nor is it a step-by-step process. It's a way of thinking or being. Consider yourself a problem-solving zen warrior with a deep philosophical foundation built on this concept.

Second, it's meant to free your mind to think and explore. It's not meant to create rigidity. Yes, part of the framework involves problem solving at speed (and speed is much of the focus of this book), but another part involves being open to new ideas. Agile is exploratory. Being Agile, at least to some degree, means thinking outside the box. It means allowing for outside influence and striving to constantly see things with fresh eyes.

We will be covering the tactical repercussions that flow from this mindset in the rest of the book, but for now, root out your preconceptions about solving problems and adjust them to be more Agile.

A Brief History of Agile Thinking

The reality is that the history of Agile thinking is the history of modern business. In 1799, Eli Whitney introduced interchangeable parts into his cotton gin, and about a century later, in 1913, Henry Ford introduced the production line that would become a staple of modern production. Both of these innovations came as direct results of being open to outside influences during problem solving. Then, after World War II at the end of the 1940s, the Toyota Production System was developed and implemented, beginning Toyota's long and epic rise to the upper echelons of the automotive manufacturing industry. Successors to the company's founder, Sakichi Toyoda, incorporated the methodologies of American W. Edwards Deming to bring the system known as TPS to international fame.

The core concepts behind all of these manufacturing advancements—the production line, just-in-time manufacturing, one-piece flow, the Kanban system and Kaizen—all had profound effects, not only in manufacturing environments, but also in offices and organizations around the world that were looking to make production more efficient and higher in quality. And again, all of these innovations were created as a result of Agile thinking. They used new ideas and impactful data to innovate instead of simply following old ways of working.

Enter the computer. As the workforce changed and industries developed around computer programming, the "Agile Manifesto" emerged as a natural response. A group of computer programmers, weary of issues they saw in the old ways of managing software projects, took concepts from the TPS, Lean manufacturing, Deming and their own experiences to form a new approach to software projects that they termed Agile development. They didn't know it at the time, but their manifesto would serve as the archetypal problem-solving framework that leaders would be using for years to come in the digital age.

The Agile revolution overhauled the American approach to project management, and really, to problem solving in general in corporate America. And Agile is still on the rise.

What do we take from all of this? Well, you don't really need to know all the ins and outs of Agile (though you'll find some resources in the appendix if you are interested). But you should understand that the complexity of problems we face today necessitates a better approach to problem solving than the one most businesses are still using. Rapid thinking and the efficient execution of possible solutions are

the keys to success. This isn't my own concoction; the proof is in the progressive innovation Agile has wrought across business contexts. However, in the hopes of removing any lingering preconceptions you have of Agile once and for all, I'm going to stop using the term from this point on and will refer to it simply as rapid thinking and execution.

What is important for you to understand is that you must change the way you think from a long-focused, linear process into a short, rapidly executed one. You should think in problem-solving cycles that are strung together like links on a chain.

This is the nature of problem solving in our rapidly changing world. Analyze the problem, try a solution and review the results. Think of it as the scientific method on steroids. Think, try, review. Whatever you want to call it, start seeing the challenges around you not as problems to be solved once and for all in a single shot, but as progressing decisions that, made wisely, will lead you step by step toward a better destination.

The Best Ideas Don't Take Very Long

You may be thinking to yourself, "Well, this all sounds great, but does rapid thinking really work? I mean, can we really do great work without doing a considerable amount of planning?"

Or, "How much planning do we really need?"

To answer these questions, consider two contexts.

The Business Plan

First, let's revisit the previous discussion of business plans. A recent study looked at 160 businesses as they progressed from start-ups to success stories (or failures).[3] The results showed that the businesses that created written business plans were generally more successful than non-planning businesses. However, the study also showed that the companies that created formal plans did so mainly *to navigate financing*. Business plans were drafted to satisfy the bankers, not to establish priorities and direct the organization's work. Overall, these businesses attributed their success more often to factors outside of their written plans than they did to the plans themselves. These businesses did not fail to plan, but they didn't over-plan, either. They simply knew how much planning was needed and acted accordingly.

This case illustrates the reality that ideas are raw, untidy and, generally, cheap. It's easy to think of an idea, but to bring an idea successfully to fruition, you need to plan at an appropriate level of detail. This means avoiding both overplanning *and* underplanning.

Marshmallow Tower

The marshmallow tower is an exercise that's widely used to teach how rapid thinking and pro-totyping can yield greater success. The premise is simple: Teams are given about two dozen pieces of dry spaghetti, a bit of tape and bit of string. They're assigned the goal of using these materials to create a structure that lifts a big marshmallow as high as possible, and they're told that they must do this in a brief amount of time, usually about 10 minutes.

At the starting bell, teams enter excitedly into conversation, talking about their plans. Leadership in the group is established, ideas are discussed, deci-sions made. It looks like a normal day at the office.

Here's the rub: Most of these corporate teams fail to even get a tower raised. There are a multitude of reasons for this, but there are three core issues.

First, most teams spend *too long in the planning process* casting a vision for the ideal tower. Then, they spend the rest of the time allotted for construction crafting impressive structures of spaghetti sticks. It's only in the last few seconds that the typical corporate team goes to place their marshmallow on the top of their tower—and when they do, they usually find that its sugary weight crushes their structures before their eyes at the ending bell. You see, the plans that they make are simply that: plans. They never give themselves a chance to test their plans against real-world data— meaning, the actual weight of the marshmallow. There's no time for iteration, and so these teams never make it to the feedback stage. They rely heavily on a plan that has more inherent uncertainty than they realize.

Second, they *only bring to the table what they know*. This is another challenge in problem solving. Leaders and members simply bring ideas from previous experience. Shapes and solutions are generally based on they've done before, even though most of their knowledge is probably completely unrelated to the problem at hand! While they've never built anything with spaghetti, they still tend to believe their solutions will work.

Third, group hierarchy is fixed in the first few minutes, and *leadership is often assumed by unqualified individuals.* Being the CEO at a business has nothing to do with lifting a marshmallow with spaghetti sticks, but our human nature responds strongly to existing social cues.

You know which group of contestants is the best at this challenge? Corporate CEOs, maybe? Engineers? You'd be wrong. If you guessed recent kindergarten graduates, you'd be right.

The reasons for this are actually quite simple. First, kids come with fewer preconceived notions about what success should look like. They plan less. They just start building. They might have a basic tower completed in two minutes.

Second, their "beginner" mindset aids them as they think about ways to approach the challenge. They rely on experimentation, not existing knowledge. They get a tower constructed early on, then make it bigger. They get farther because they rely on real-world feedback to verify their approaches.

And third, they don't have highly structured social groups. More ideas are considered valid and open to experimentation. They work together to accomplish the mission without the social hinderances of authority and rank.

As you begin to examine your own problem-solving approaches, this experiment is instructive because it illustrates some of the biggest issues endemic to the corporate world. Processes are clouded by over planning, old thinking and irrelevant authority. You need to adapt a method of working that removes these barriers so that you can achieve greater results. Especially in your marketing.

Both the marshmallow challenge and the current state of the business plan show that good ideas should be generated and iterated rapidly. Ideas can't be validated by detailed plans. Instead, the validation of a "good" idea happens as the idea is executed, tested and evaluated. You must be willing to give up the preconception that good ideas take a long time to create. The data shows that good ideas can emerge very quickly. So your goal should be to get your ideas into the market rapidly to prove their worth, rather than relying on the validation of your own internal approvals.

Minimal Investment to Return

Let's tackle one final aspect of rapid thinking and execution before we dig more deeply into how this leads to a new framework for marketing.

We desire perfection before we launch initiatives, but the goal of this new way of problem solving isn't perfection—

it's results.

We've covered a variety of concepts so far, and you've probably found yourself consistently asking the same question: "How much is enough?"

* *How much planning should we do before we test our ideas out?*

* *How much execution should we do before we stop to evaluate what's working?*

* *How much should we spend before we expect to see results?*

All of these are good questions. Generally speaking, the goal of nearly any business process is to maximize a return and/or minimize a cost. In rapid thinking and executing, returns generally fall into one of two categories: direct financial returns or insight-based returns. For instance, rapid thinking may allow you to generate more sales. Or, rapid execution might result in data or knowledge that has intrinsic value to your business, such as intellectual property you can sell outright or turn into a new product or service. In any case, wherever you are employing rapid thinking and execution, you should clearly define what you hope to achieve with it and what you expect a successful return to look like.

START SMALL. START WITH AN MVP.

Cost should be the other consideration. What action will be required to generate what you'd consider a successful return? Remember, all actions have a cost. Even if it's not a direct cost of capital, what you do can always be measured in time or labor. To answer the question, "How much is enough?" you have to clarify what return you're looking for and what you're willing to pay. If you clarify both of these things, you'll know when you're reached the results you desire or when you've spent as much as you're willing to pay—and at that point, it's enough.

Your goal, of course, is to generate more return than cost. The brilliance of acting fast is that you can validate the effectiveness of your actions before you incur too high a cost. For example, if you created a detailed plan to spend all $30K of your advertising budget on a single channel and then find in execution that you've spread your investment too thin in the wrong places—well, you're straight out of luck. But, if you spend $1–2K of your budget in targeted ways and evaluate the different rates of return as you do so, you'll be able to double down on what works and maximize your returns. Sounds great, right?

In the product world, the first working version is called the minimally viable product, or the MVP. It's the product that's sufficient for entering a market and collecting consumer feedback.

To co-opt that term and apply it to marketing, an MVP is a minimally viable program—the version of *a marketing strategy that requires the least amount of investment to generate actionable results.* It's built as an answer to the question, "What are the lowest-cost concepts and tactics we can use to test the validity of our ideas?"

For some leaders, the idea of an MVP is incredibly uncomfortable. Taking an MVP approach means creating campaign elements with minimal planning and cohesion, and that might seem fragmented to some thinkers. Some marketers hold tightly to an expectation that certain things must exist in concert to be effective, or to the belief that things must be of a certain caliber before they see the light of day. The idea that they might "try" something before coming up with the final product runs against their core beliefs.

For these individuals, MVP thinking is hard. Could they launch a one-page website before launching the entire thing? Could they start with only three service pages when the website's full specifications call for six? Could they implement cold calling scripts to see how they work with a select audience of potential customers without doing the dialing themselves?

We desire perfection before we launch initiatives, but the goal of this new way of problem solving isn't perfection—it's results.

Developing a good MVP is critical in order to successfully iterate on your solutions. There are a few things that make an MVP "good." First, good MVPs are developed with clearly defined standards for what they're expected to reveal or yield—in other words, with returns in mind. Second, they are developed with an understanding of the minimal investment that will be needed to prove their viability. You can't say that Google Search ads don't work if you only spend $10, for example; an MVP must account for costs realistically.

Finally, keep in mind that good MVPs must be able to be tested and improved. For example, you could spend $200 on a particular advertising channel to see what return your investment brings. Then, you could try the same spend two or three more times using different content to see if you can change the rate of return. A good MVP must allow you to move forward.

Jim Collins summarizes the concept of MVPs in his book, *Good to Great*, using the metaphor of firing bullets before cannons. The concept, as he explains it, is that many companies will fire cannons (large investments or energy and capital) at a target, only to miss due to poor projections or inaccurate evaluations of the marketplace. He suggests firing bullets (smaller, focused investments) until you hit the target. Once you hit the target, then you can fire the cannon. This metaphor explains the MVP in a nutshell. Fire bullets, then bigger bullets, then cannons.

Start small. Start with an MVP.

MVPs are a key to rapid thinking and executing. Seek clear paths to incremental returns and pursue actions that are focused on achieving long-term goals. The MVP is the vehicle of action that will drive your solutions from one iteration to the next.

MOVING INTO THE RTX FRAMEWORK

At this point, you should have a solid understanding of the concepts and ideas that you must bring with you into this new marketing framework in order to use it effectively. Once you understand the strategic foundation of rapid thinking and acting, the RTX Framework that flows from it is quite simple. Before we take the next step, let's quickly review our concepts.

Kill the long-term plan.

Don't allow long-term thinking to blind you to the reality of uncertainty. Think iteratively. Plan and act in shorter bursts, learning and improving along the way.

Be nimble.

An Agile mindset is the key. Let go of the need for a clear path to the end, because your idealized plan is a fallacy. Instead, replace your preconceived thoughts with the scientific method. Think, act, evaluate, repeat. Do this in shorter timeframes.

Think, but don't overthink.

Allow ideas to come quickly, and don't discount the ones that are simple. Create options, think outside of box, and don't let your organization, structure or people get in the way. Remember: A good idea is not a good idea until it's validated!

Do just enough.

As you move into the RTX Framework, you'll be planning and acting in smaller bursts. It's important to do just enough to get relevant results. You can use those results to plan another campaign that will improve on them. In the parlance of Jim Collins, fire bullets, then cannons.

With these concepts in mind, you are ready to enter the marketing framework and start riding the tornado of change.

THE RTX FRAMEWORK

Welcome to the framework that will change the way your company approaches marketing and innovation forever.

That's a big statement. But, as you'll see, this is more than just a way to do marketing. It's a framework through which you can accomplish goals and innovate in every aspect of your organization. Marketing and innovation can lead you to overcome the biggest challenges that businesses like yours face, and this framework can help you leverage the great opportunities you have in any area of your business.

THE THREE STAGES
OF THE FRAMEWORK

The RTX Framework exists in three stages. They are sequential in the sense that there is a logical progression to carrying them out. You can't, for example, ideate, skip execution and go right to assessment; you need to execute so that you have data to assess. But there is no beginning and there is no end. You can simply enter into the cycle wherever you might be in your current marketing process and move forward from there. If you do have the choice, though, the phase that functions best as a starting point is the Assessment Stage.

The three stages are:

Assessment: This is your reflection and analysis stage. It's where you analyze your data, compile your findings and create the insight that you'll use to generate ideas.

Ideation: This stage is focused on generating ideas to be acted on. It's where you brainstorm the tactics, activities and strategies that you'll execute.

Execution: This is the stage where you act on your ideas. You'll launch campaigns and drive results, making the most of your investments in time and capital so that you'll have data to assess.

As you can see, this is a fairly simple approach to marketing. But it can be complex to employ effectively. The good news is that each time you complete a cycle, you'll get better at the very process of completing a cycle. Each revolution creates learning and improves the skill of participants in carrying out the processes. Together, the three stages encircle a goal, the axis around which all activity and thinking rotate.

As you practice this approach, you start to sense the "zen" of it. Again, this is more a mindset for growth than it is a box of specific tools.

Goals: The Eye of the Tornado

If you have a desire to improve your business, you've likely identified two things: the current state of your business and the future state you desire your business to reach. The gap between these two states is the place where this journey begins. Starting here, you will clarify your goals and begin a revolution that moves you toward them, changing your business and your marketing for the better.

Now, you're not here to read a pep talk on the importance of setting goals, so we'll skip some of the pomp and nuance. There are lots of other resources to help with goal setting, a few of which are listed in the appendix. But for this framework to have any value, it's critical that you do *have* a goal. Your goal is the center of all of this. It's the key ingredient.

You cannot use this rapid thinking and execution framework without a clear desired outcome. What would the point be? You can assess, ideate and execute anything—the color you choose to paint your walls, or the way you comb your hair or the number of chairs that you have in your office—but unless there's a reason to *improve* something, this tool will have little value to you. Without a goal, you'll just be spinning your wheels uselessly.

That's because you can't know where to start if you don't know where you are. If you don't have data on your position yet, that is okay for now. You'll get the data soon enough. But you must have some kind of before-and-after picture you are working from that will give you at least a start toward defining your goals. For example, if you are spending $50K a year on marketing and are not yielding any leads, that is a tough (but accurate) starting point, and you can turn it into a goal. Perhaps you'll create a goal to turn that $50K into 30 new clients. Now you are speaking the right language.

If you're fairly new to goal setting in your business, I'd recommend that you use the SMART goal framework. SMART is an acronym that stands for Specific, Measurable, Actionable, Realistic and Timely. There is a more detailed explanation in Appendix A. Following a SMART goal framework will allow you to create clear goals—the kind of goals that this framework will help you to achieve. No matter what goal you center this process around, keeping the goal in focus at the center of everything is critical to your success.

Eyes on the prize.

Once you have a goal (or several), you've started the journey toward your future state. The process we are about to enter will require you to go "heads-down"

Your goal is the eye of your tornado. Keep it at the center and jump right in.

and focus on specific metrics and actions. You'll get pulled into the day-to-day and might even start to enjoy all of the activity that it brings. But it is important that, in every stage of the framework, you come up for air. You must come back to the goal and measure your progress against the goal each time you plot your next steps.

Without alignment toward a goal, short-term cycles of activity can take you off course. Even veteran marketers aren't immune to getting caught up in results and taking their eyes off the ultimate goal. Progress can be exhilarating. Results can prompt a lot of high-fives in sales meetings. Those things are good, but don't forget to come back to your goals and keep moving toward your final destination.

Your goal is the eye of your tornado. Keep it at the center and jump right in.

Stage: Assess

THE ASSESSMENT STAGE

The purpose of the Assessment Stage is to look with a critical eye at the data generated from the Execution Stage in order to determine how effectively your efforts are achieving your desired outcomes. We assess to figure out what's working and what isn't working. You can do this by looking at your existing data or creating new data to review. Everyone has data, and in this section we'll talk about what types of data you want to track.

How This Stage Interacts with the Ideation Stage

The Assessment Stage is the precursor to the Ideation Stage. Data generates valuable insight about your performance as a company, and you can achieve even better results in the future by accounting for that insight as you plan for your next cycle.

The Assessment Stage also answers a lot of questions—questions like: Is social media going to produce what we need? Is our email list valid? The answers will help guide the next Ideation Stage and then the next Execution Stage, giving you a foundation on which to build your future marketing strategies. Of course, the answers to your questions also tend to create more questions.

How This Stage Interacts with the Execution Stage

The Assessment Stage comes immediately after the Execution Stage. As you leave the Execution Stage, you're in retrospection. Often, you'll have successes to celebrate, along with great data that makes you excited about planning your projects. In other cases, the Execution Stage fails to generate positive results, or fails even to generate the data you need to clearly determine *why* results weren't achieved. Could it have been flawed execution? Could you have made the wrong move entirely? Failure means you'll have a lot more digging to do to understand what happened and why. In these cases, the Assessment Stage tends to be more like a C.S.I. postmortem rather than a locker room party after winning the big game. Either way, after execution, assessment is critical.

Assessment of the Tactics

This phase is called the Assessment Stage because its goal is to *make a judgement* about the strategies and tactics you've used in your marketing efforts. This is more than simply analysis, which is to break a whole into understandable parts—although you'll do that in this phase. It is also more than just evaluation, although you'll to determine how close your activities brought you to hitting your goals. Assessment involves a verdict. So, your ultimate aim is to generate **insight**: a judgement that will inform your actions for the next phase of your marketing efforts.

Starting with the Data

Data is ground zero where the tornado touches down—the foundation of your goals, measurements and activities. Everything you do should allow you to create, collect or interpret relevant data.

There are many types of marketing data available to most marketers. Some more custom data could be acquired through deeper measurement, but most of you should have access to the following without much configuration.

* Website Analytics; Visitor Data, Sessions Data, and Page Data

* CRM; Contact Data, Interaction Data

* Email; Open Rates, Click-Thru Rates, Sequence Data

* Social Media; Follower Data; Post Data

* Paid Media; Costs, ROI, Placements

* Conversions; Source, Value, Consideration Path

Accordingly, during the Assessment Stage, you first need to evaluate the relevancy of your data by asking the question: "Does our data set allow us to evaluate the metrics supporting our goal?" Or, put another way: "Do we have the right data to create a reasonable and accurate picture of what it will take to achieve our goal?"

Without context, this question is a bit abstract, so let's make it more tangible with an example to show where you might have a gap in your data. Let's say that you are using an email campaign to try to generate leads. What data might you have, and what data might you need, in order to make decisions that will support your goal?

Most obviously, you would have all of your email campaign data. You would see common metrics inside your email marketing platform, like open rates, click-through rates, unsubscribes, bounces— all of the data that your email service provider would generate. Importantly, though, this data would not be enough to fully assess email's impact on your goal of generating leads. It would only be enough data to analyze your tactic. You might see, for example, that you have driven 80 clicks to your campaign landing page from your email, yet have little data as to what happened to those people when they reached the page. You might have had a few folks submit the form on your landing page, but that does not *conclusively* show that they were the same ones who clicked your emails. To determine how effective email is, you need to have data that shows the traffic on your landing page with attribution (that is, where the traffic comes from) so that you can draw a straight line from the tactic to your goal of leads.

The point is that to properly evaluate an activity, you might need more data than the activity alone generates. You will probably need to evaluate secondary or supporting metrics in order to really assess your activity's success.

This leads to a second question: Did you collect enough data? If you fell into the problem outlined above, the answer might be no. Luckily, in our example, you might have access to attribution data in a platform like Google Analytics, so it would be easy to go back and gather the data needed to form an assessment.

In other cases, though, the data you need might be inaccessible. Or—and this can be more challenging—you may find that the dataset you're measuring doesn't conclusively prove anything. You may assume that a specific metric is correlated to an outcome when, in fact, it is not.

Behavioral and demographic measurements, for example, are commonly confused. You might have grown your social media channel by 200 followers over your last marketing cycle, exceeding your goal of 150. Way to go! Except, as it turns out, 200 followers is a count of membership, not of engagement. You set this goal because you assumed that followers would correlate to sales, but you are not seeing the sales come in. What is going on? Well, your followers might be fake. Or they might be your friends. Or they might be fake friends. Regardless, it seems clear that one thing they are *not* is your target buyer. In other words, you have measured a dataset that is inconclusive because you have assumed a correlation that does not necessarily exist. While you've achieved your goal, you cannot know if your campaign was successful because the metric of follower count may be the wrong thing to track—at least, until you're able to qualify what good followers mean in more detail.

This example also demonstrates another important reality. As you execute your marketing cycles, you need to be exact in specifying the data you are looking for to measure success. In the example above, success was not just 200 followers. But it might have been 200 followers who fit your buyer persona. Maybe you shouldn't track 100 visitors to your website; maybe you should track 100 targeted visitors to your website who enter on a specific page. Drilling down is a crucial task in creating *useful* data that will help you assess the success of your activities.

So, deeply consider whether you have all of the relevant data points you will need to determine success. If you did not collect the data you think you need, then ask, "Why?" There are plenty of reasons why this may have happened, and you should take steps to correct any issues that you find. But it's also important to remember that you are using this process to iterate, improve and move toward your goals. It can be all right to clearly identify what you are lacking so that you can correct it in the future, ensuring that next time you execute, you'll have the ability to collect the right data. Yet don't fall short. Always look for more data and be vigilant about specifying what the right data is. The right data will lead to the insight that will change the course of your results.

People, Process, Tactics

The second part of the Assessment Stage is to take the data you have collected and understand what it says about the people, processes and tactics involved in your approach. Once you have a flow of data, you can start looking upstream to determine what factors influenced it. This is where you will start to judge how operations could be improved.

The best way to do this part of the Assessment Stage is to hold a one-hour team meeting. Once the data is collected, you will have a result set to discuss, and you can gather feedback on the success or failure of the Execution Stage. Bring the team into the conversation to discuss the data and to evaluate what it says about your people, processes and tactics. Focus on:

PEOPLE

People are the hardest factor to analyze. Their performances can wax and wane. They get distracted. They have great days and bad days. Accordingly, people are often a core part of any issues or successes in the execution of tactics. Attracting and developing a strong team is obviously essential to developing a successful company, and this book is not intended to be a human resources manual. But this much is clear: If a person was assigned an activity with a reasonable benchmark and clear directions, yet still failed, you need to have a conversation with them. There may be missing information that explains a lack of results, but you need to conclusively determine whether they have the ability to handle the role for the next cycle. If the directions they were given were not clear or the approach they were assigned was not effective, then you have a process problem.

You'll find that the common factors impacting failure (a lack of knowledge, a lack of capability and a lack of time) are all tied to people. So, during the Assessment Stage, be sure to evaluate each one of these dimensions with your team to make sure that you have the right people on the right tactics.

PROCESS AND TOOLS

Next, look at your processes and tools to see if they aided or encumbered the mission. It's best to think of a process as a play in an NFL playbook. When the player knows the play, and the play gets him open but he drops the ball, then the failure is on the player. However, if the team calls a passing play in a situation where they should have called a run, then the failure rests on the playbook—or, in this case, the process.

So, take the time to evaluate the process and each person's role in its execution, because this will help to determine the root cause of performance issues. It will also allow for productive conversation that will lead into the Ideation Stage. Your team will likely have ideas about what can be improved in the process to get better results next time. Look at all aspects of the process; analyze even the communication with the project management team.

Also, you should look at your tools. These might include the software and hardware you're using to get the job done. After you see all the data, you might realize that you need to try new tools to improve efficiency or accuracy in your execution. The appropriate tools can have a major impact on outcomes.

TACTICS

The last discussion, which will ultimately shape the process moving forward, should center around the tactics themselves. If you've followed the process so far, you have data that shows whether or not your tactic produced the result you wanted. Yet, as we've discussed, your data might not tell the whole story. This is the point of having the team review the tactic together; the meeting allows you to discuss all attendant factors and may lead you to uncover information that you wouldn't have realized without group input. This discussion should be open, so that team members are able to discuss people, processes, tools and tactics directly and freely. If you embrace the cycle fully, you'll find that your team is more open to admitting fault, since members know that a subpar outcome can mean an adjustment of a process or approach. A lack of success is not a death sentence.

Organizing Data into Assessment Tools

Taking your assessment to the next level requires building tools that will enhance your ability to collect and track data throughout the entirety of the cycle. Assessment is a particular phase of the cycle, certainly; yet each stage of the cycle will generate data that should be used to assess the cycle and improve it as it goes forward.

There is not a single part of the process that does not involve the collection or review of data, so having a good way to track data from all phases of your journey is important to your long-term success. Tools are also powerful ways to organize data into formats that are more likely to generate insight and create a narrative or visual picture of how your process is working. Tools provide a touchpoint to help everyone on the team understand the big picture of the goal and monitor progress toward it.

DASHBOARDS (SCORECARDS)

The most essential tool for data tracking is the scorecard. The scorecard is a simple tool that tracks the leading indicators that are executed in pursuit of the goal. It should also track progress toward the goal itself—although this is a lag indicator, it is helpful in maintaining focus.

The value of the scorecard is that it is updated in real time throughout the execution process, allowing for iteration and feedback to happen as you execute. The scorecard doesn't have to update every second, but rather at an interval that will provide the team with actionable feedback.

Using a scorecard to track leading indicators in real time will allow your team to clearly measure progress against your goal. You'll gain actionable management direction to guide the people, processes and tactics that are happening inside the Execution Stage. We'll cover ways to build a scorecard in the next section; for now, the key takeaway is that you need to track data at every stage of your process.

What Data Do You Already Have?

Of course, you may simply not have the right data. Data is the bedrock of objective decision making and should be the lens through which you view all aspects of your organization. It prevents biased assumptions.

As you problem solve, recognize that in the gap between your current and ideal results is a wide field of "gray space" occupied by myriad data points called indicators. These indicators are barometers as you move closer to your objectives, and you should use them to evaluate how far along you are in your problem solving—to find out how close you are from "here" to "there."

So once you identify your problem, the next question to answer is: What data points or indicators can you track to measure your progress toward the solution? These indicators will tell the story of your progress, and they will help your team move the right levers in the machine to get the right results.

It's important to note that one of the most common errors in indicator tracking is to track lag indicators instead of lead indicators. **Lag indicators** are data points that are the result of some action or process; net profit, for example, is a lag indicator. You can't affect net profit directly. You would have to break it down into the categories of "expenses" or "income" to start seeing avenues for action. These are worthwhile metrics to track, certainly, but their place is to demonstrate results, not progress.

Lead indicators, on the other hand, are data points that you *can* impact directly. These are factors like number of sales calls, budget spent on search ads or hours spent on research. They're metrics that you can impact directly to progress toward your goals.

Many times, marketers use lag indicators to track progress when they should be using lead indicators to solve a problem. For example, you may try to solve a website traffic problem by monitoring the number of users to the site each month. But you can't directly impact website traffic; you'd do better to track a traffic generation *tactic* that you could impact.

As you discuss which indicators to track, make sure that you are measuring lead indicators to track your progress. You can (and should) still use lag indicators to measure outcomes.

It's also important to think deeply about whether data is simply available or truly actionable. Just because data is available doesn't mean you should use it. With a critical eye, ask yourself, "How does this data help us to solve the problem?" When you ask this question, you'll often realize that the data you are reviewing is simply *there*; it doesn't provide any actionable insights that influence your next steps in reaching your goal. It might very well remind you how far behind your goals you are, but if it's not giving you a clear path forward, don't track it.

You might find after a deeper review that you need better data. In fact, as you begin using this framework, that will usually be the case, and it likely will be for several cycles. There are two reasons for this: First, your data might be disorganized—while you might have good data, it isn't formatted or organized in ways that will bring insight. If this is the case, then you need to develop the right tools to organize and analyze it. Second, you may not have the right data at all. In this case, you can backtrack or plan for better data capture on the next Execution Stage so that you don't run into the same issue next time. Either way, getting the right data for your Ideation Stage is critical in creating better ideas and outcomes.

Leaving the Assessment Stage

The assessment stage is a critical pause point in the cycle, because it is usually the stage in which you decide to continue, start or stop your process toward a goal. Your retrospection here should allow you to consider if continuing is worth it. Making the decision about how to move forward takes a considerable effort and shouldn't be done lightly. You may, on the other hand, just be starting the process; in this case, you're assessing without previous execution. If this is so, then the way you structure your data collection will positively influence the Ideation Stage. You'll certainly be in a better position than you would be if you started in the Ideation Stage and began by brainstorming and blindly executing without paying any mind to data collection.

How Do Your Current Results Compare to the Projection?

You have a goal, and you either are hitting it or you are not. The value of a well-defined goal is that it leaves little ambiguity as to your success. If you hit your goal, it's a simple decision to keep going or to switch and focus on another goal.

If you did not hit the goal, you have another decision to make, one that is quite a bit harder.

The first thing you should consider is how far away you were from reaching your goal. Sometimes, being close is a really good sign. If you were shooting for eight new leads per month and you achieved an average of six after getting none a year ago, you're in a better place. On the other hand, if you had the same goal and only hit one lead, your ROI is likely to be far too low to consider pursuing the same efforts moving forward.

Taking the time to really think through your results and calculate the ROI of your activities can help you to evaluate your goal, as well. Can you hit it as you grow going forward? The thing to consider here is your trajectory. Are you on the right one? Are you plateauing? Are you declining? If you invest a little more effort or time, do you believe that you will hit the goal you are looking for?

What Critical Issues Were Discovered?

In this analysis, you might have uncovered some valuable insights into the way your people and processes impacted performance; you may have identified problems that you believe can be solved, giving you great hope in the potential for better results next time. Two questions you have to answer now: Can you fix them easily? And how will fixing problems impact your ROI?

If you need to make a few simple changes to the process, that is a great outcome, and it probably means it is worth it to carry your goal and activities forward. But if your team is asking for an $800,000 training program for a new piece of software, solving the issues may not give you the ROI you need to continue.

Measures Versus Meaning?

The last question you should answer before you move forward is this: Are you gaining insight? In other words, are you just tracking data, or are you getting smarter? The essential byproduct of this entire cycle is that you get smarter.

"Getting smarter" means that you are developing insight; insight means you are able to *see inside*. Are you able to see inside your marketing and efforts with greater clarity now? Can you identify which actions create which results? Does the goal seem more achievable or less achievable now?

Insight is generally reliant on the creation of your own data. Your data should give you a benchmark to measure against. It should become proprietary, an asset that you can now bring into the Ideation Stage as you brainstorm the activities and tactics you will use to pursue your goals.

At this point, you may alternatively realize that you have a gap in your data. You don't have insight, so you can't make heads or tails of what you've just completed. You are just as unsure of cause and effect in your marketing as you were before.

This reality check should cause you to go deeper as you assess your data, processes and people. You should search for meaning inside your activities and data, so that you have some foothold to propel your next cycle toward different and more accurate results. The core lesson for you to understand is that you are trying to achieve something you haven't achieved before. Expect it to be a challenge and allow yourself to iterate as you continually use the cycle. Expect failures. Yet don't fail to learn and gather insight each time you complete the cycle, so that you can complete it more successfully the next time.

Stage: Ideation

THE IDEATION STAGE

The goal of the ideation stage is to generate ideas, concepts and actions to move you toward your goal.

How This Stage Interacts with the Execution Stage

The ideation stage precedes the execution stage; it will give birth to all of the concepts and possible actions that you'll pursue next. It goes without saying that you should always think before you act (unless, of course, you prefer dramatic outcomes).

The Ideation Stage provides the direction for activities in the Execution Stage. This is not to say that no decision making happens in the Execution Stage, but the Ideation Stage will create the guidelines for execution. For example, ideation could lead to the decision to create a paid social media campaign; execution might lead to the decision to try a different variation of an ad.

The ideas that seem most likely to succeed are elevated to the Execution Stage for the next cycle. The other concepts and ideas that are generated but not chosen should be documented for reference in the following cycles. Remember, the environment

Insight

IS THE PRIMARY DELIVERABLE OF THE ASSESSMENT STAGE, AND

EVERY BIT OF IT SHOULD BE USED WITH FERVOR IN THE

Ideation Stage.

and your organization are constantly changing. What doesn't work today may be worth trying tomorrow.

How This Stage Interacts with the Assessment Stage

The ideation stage is highly reliant on many forms of information and data—such as tribal or colloquial information, historical data, industry data, analytics pertaining to your market, or budgetary and financial data. There can and should be a wide array of information that is borrowed from other disciplines and studies. But the assessment stage provides a key piece to the ideation stage that no other source can offer: insight.

Insight is the distillation of information into a principle that influences future direction. For example, an insight from data might be that searches for one of your services increase by 3X in a particular month due to seasonal variations; to get specific, let's say you're in HVAC and see a measurable increase in searches for "furnace repair" during January. This insight would prove helpful in the Ideation Stage as you evaluate which tactics to execute; when January rolls around, you'll know that an opportunity exists.

Insight is the primary deliverable of the Assessment Stage, and every bit of it should be used with fervor in the Ideation Stage.

What Is the Problem, Really?

The Ideation Stage is the great "conversation stage" of the cycle. This is because the ideation stage requires the clear articulation of the problem that must be overcome to reach the goal.

Without a clear understanding of the problem (and the factors that contribute to the problem), you cannot begin to propose solutions. If you attempt to solve a problem that you don't understand, you run the risk of solving the wrong problem. You may set a course that will lead you not to your goal, but to what *looks like* your goal, but doesn't produce the results you need.

There are a few ways that you can make sure you are defining the problem correctly. Let's cover a few core questions that you can ask to ensure you're finding the root problem, so that you can generate the right ideas for how to solve it.

Answering Questions with Questions

Sometimes, when you hear a person state a problem, your natural response is to start to solve the problem

A SIMPLE EXERCISE TO TEST THIS ASSUMPTION IS TO ASK THE "5 WHYS." BY ASKING "WHY?" MULTIPLE TIMES IN

SUCCESSION, YOU CAN START TO DIG DEEPER INTO THE TRUE PROBLEM. EVENTUALLY, YOU'LL GET TO AN UNDERLYING "WHY."

as stated. This response does two things: First, it moves the conversation into problem-solving mode very quickly, which can lead you toward misdirected activity. Second, it fails to determine whether the problem that's been stated is the *true* problem.

A simple exercise to test this assumption is to ask the "5 Whys." By asking "why?" multiple times in succession, you can start to dig deeper into the true problem. Eventually, you'll get to an underlying "why."

For example, your sales team might say, "The problem is that we don't have enough leads." You can respond with the first, "why?" They might answer, "Because our lists are old," or, "Because we're too busy to do more prospecting."

There! You've now uncovered issues and problems that are more granular and actionable.

Here's another example: "Email marketing doesn't work for us." (You can replace email marketing with any type of marketing.) You might then ask, "Why doesn't it work?" You'll likely get responses that have nothing to do with email marketing itself like, "It costs too much", or "Bill tried it once and nothing happened", or "We're too busy to do it well right now".

The rationale here is to *ask more questions before you accept your problems at face value.* This is key to starting your Ideation Stage. Without a true and deep understanding of your problems, you run the risk of solving the wrong problem and wasting time and energy.

Problem to Be Solved or a Tension to Be Managed?

Ask yourself the question, "Is this a problem that can be solved or is it really a tension to be managed?"

For example, let's say that the sales team thinks that the marketing team doesn't provide good leads, yet the marketing team thinks that the sales team can't close leads. There is a pile of social and team issues in this scenario, of course, but the underlying reality is that both teams may be partly right and there may be no solution to the problem. There may only be expectations and nuances to be managed, but you can work with both sides to solve minor issues around the main tension and create better results.

How Are Others Solving It?

As you work through ideation, consider where your ideas are coming from. How big is your universe of solutions? Two people who have been in your industry for 30 years might have a really narrow universe of solutions for your problems. Their own experiences might function as blinders, getting in the way of their ability to find innovative solutions.

This is a huge leadership opportunity. Don't be afraid to identify new and innovative solutions to add to your universe. One simple way to do this is to research how others are solving your problem—and not just others in your industry, but others in adjacent industries, too. This will take research. You might allow for a longer Ideation Stage because you'll need to take the time to research whether what's in the market could work for you.

Legend has it that Henry Ford developed the basis of his production line by watching hog slaughtering in inner-city Chicago. He saw how the processes made work more efficient; output was greater when one individual did one task repeatedly than it was when one person performed multiple tasks.

You should follow his example and search other industries and even your competitors. Look for insights and core truths that might make parts of your job easier. Don't let blinders limit your openness to innovation.

Maybe your problem truly is unique. But remember that the intent of a free market economy is to provide solutions to common problems so that we all can thrive. Don't assume no one has solved your problem before.

Lastly, as you look at solutions, you should evaluate each for its cost-to-benefit ratio. Sometimes, the solutions in the marketplace offer 150% of what you need for your MVP. You may need one feature, only to find that to get it, you have to pay for eight others. This is one of the bigger challenges in the cycle. Take the cost seriously and use it as a data point in your ideation so that you can best match your solution to your goal.

Most Issues Are Caused by People

If you have a service business, most of your issues are caused by your people. It's a hard pill to swallow, but it really is the truth. You don't have machines to blame or suppliers to chastise; issues nearly always come down to your own team. Don't let the buck be passed too easily to outside forces. Look to your own team to be part of any issue (if not the majority of it).

When you do identify a people issue, you could take dramatic action and remove someone—but often, people issues are nuanced and solutions don't require removal. You might need to augment your staff with contract employees or vendors, or provide training for the member at the root of the issue.

What Data Do You Have for the Problem?

It's a gross understatement to say that if you don't look at data, you're making bad decisions. Daniel Kahenman, noted behavioral physiologist, talks about the human brain's "noise level"—our tendency to incorporate meaningless data into our decision-making processes without realizing it. A doctor might be more likely to offer a mild diagnosis when the sun is shining, for example, even though the weather would have no impact on a case. Kahenman's solution to avoiding bad decisions is to ground decisions in data. The key thing to remember is that, no matter how self-aware you are, your brain will deceive you if left to its own devices—so rely on data.

If data is not at the core of your ideation stage, you need to go back to the Assessment Stage. If you don't have the data you need, you should seek it. Again, you need to make better decisions and to come up with better ideas in the next cycle. Clear data is the primary driver of good ideas. Remember, you can't even know if an idea is good (or was good) until you see its results.

If you don't have access to the data you need, then you should execute on a very short cycle so you can acquire it quickly. For example, if you want to increase conversions on your website but you don't have existing data on them, you should shorten your cycle. Set up conversion tracking and measure it for two weeks. Assess your data after the allotted time-frame and then return to ideation. Rather than acting without information, you should find out where you are first.

Lastly, any data is better than perfect data. You might not have all of the data that you'll need to fully understand your problem. You might create more questions that you'll need data to answer. Document your questions and keep them in mind as you move through the cycle, so that you'll be ready to answer them the next time around.

Benchmark data is also helpful to have as you define your problem. This means generalized indus-try data that gives you a basis for comparison to other companies in your industry. It can be helpful—but take it with a grain of salt, too. Some marketing software companies will skew data higher or lower to make your results on their software seem good. If you're on an email platform, for example, they might show you that you're "beating the industry" with your click-through rates when, in fact, you are part of another industry altogether. It's best to pull your benchmarks from third-party research organi-zations, not from vendors who have a vested interest in your business.

What Questions Need to Be Asked First?

Once you complete the cycle a few times, you'll be able to ask your own set of questions that are ideally tailored to your problems. But for the first few cycles (or even as a refresher), it's helpful to have an introductory set of questions as a reference to help in your ideation. Here are some examples:

1. **What is our current progress to the goal?**

2. **What did we learn from the last cycle?**

3. **What happened that we did not expect?**

4. **Do we see any trends in the data that we did not see before?**

5. **If we started over, what would we do differently?**

6. **Could someone else do it better?**

7. **What would the most expensive/ cheapest solutions look like?**

8. *How does our data compare to the industry's benchmarks?*

9. *How would you solve this problem with video? With email? With search ads? (Basically, test concepts on different channels.)*

10. *How does this compare to other campaigns we've run?*

11. *What is something new to try?*

Not All Problems Have Solutions

Once you have your problem clearly defined, you will likely realize the truth that defines any great problem: Initially, you will have no idea how to solve it.

If you are a Type A or C on the DISC profile, this might cause you some serious anxiety. Everyone reacts differently to this truth, and your response is what this framework is designed to address. This process exists to help you evaluate solutions rapidly and to assist you in finding the right path when you aren't sure how to move forward.

If you feel inclined to dismiss your problem as unsolvable, remember that you're simply making a knee-jerk reaction. We have a tendency to freeze or create barriers when our minds don't provide immediate answers. It takes practice to analyze your reaction to your perceived lack of options and then move toward a solution. In this section, we're going to cover some ideas to help you push into the intimidating world of unfamiliar decisions.

We Don't Have to Know Everything to Be Confident

One of the biggest hang-ups in the decision-making process is a lack of confidence in the ideas that you may have. You might not have enough data. You might have no history, no playbook and no experiences that provide context for understanding the problem. This lack of confidence in your ability to make a decision can stymie progress.

Where does that confidence come from? From both previous experience and your ability to analyze risk based on available data. To illustrate the latter, let's look at poker. In stud poker, you know your hand, but you don't know the other player's hand. The data that you have access to only represents a small part of what's happening in the game; thus, the risk is high. In Texas hold 'em, though, you get five cards down and two cards up. The data you have access to allows for more confidence; risk is greatly diminished because the unknown variables are reduced to two cards per person.

Likewise, in business, when we know the data sets that determine our risk—when we know how much we know—we can have more confidence as we enter the ideation stage.

For an additional boost of confidence, look to the principles recounted in the book *Blink* by Malcom Gladwell. The basic premise of the book is that we can evaluate a significant amount of information in a short span of time through the practice of "thin-slicing." In layman's terms, thin-slicing refers to the fact that our first impressions tend to be fairly accurate—and they get more accurate the more we know. To illustrate this, Gladwell recounts an example of an art expert who was instantly able to tell that a statue was a fake, even before knowing *why* it was a fake. This phenomenon happens because our brains can rapidly and unknowingly match what we see to previous experiences. We develop "gut" reactions very quickly, and they're often right. The basic lesson is that trusting your gut can be helpful, *if* you have a developed gut.

Likewise, in business, when we know the data sets that determine our risk—when we know how much we know—we can have more confidence as we enter the ideation stage.

Both of these examples show that the data we encounter and our perceptions of the world tend to influence us more than we think. Yet we also have the ability to perceive and process great amounts of data to make good judgements quickly. The bottom line is that the length of time we spend planning shouldn't be what inspires our confidence. There are other factors that matter much more.

What Does a Cycle Look Like?

This RTX Framework for marketing directs you to propose a solution (ideate), test it (execute) and measure the results (assess). The MVP is simply the vehicle of those tests. You might try 10 different MVPs before you solve your problem, or you might find inspiration and reach your goal in three MVPs or less.

The important thing is that you treat your MVP according to its purpose. Your insights and data shape what the MVP looks like; crafting it is like preparing a rocket payload to reach a remote planet. You plan as best as you can, prepare for worst-case scenarios with the best of intentions—and then you pack it up and wish it well as it goes out to the launch pad. The outcome of your MVP will make or break the success of your Ideation Stage.

It's also helpful to consider what your MVP will look like at different intervals in time. What does your MVP look like today? What might it look like in one week? What about in one month? And so on. This exercise is simply about challenging your team and yourself to think about how best to execute a solution within a time constraint. Constraining the time forces you and your team to think about what *needs* to happen to create successful results. One of the key steps in effective problem solving is to identify and establish constraints that will narrow down the possible outcomes of solutions. At times, to aid the problem-solving process, you can create artificial constraints to do this. At other times you might release constraints to open up additional possibilities, whether that means reimagining budget, time, resources, physics—anything, really, to spur the creative juices.

Time is usually the most impactful restraint, though. Limiting time seems to generate the greatest amount of variation in problem solving. Time constraints create unexpected solutions.

Leaving the Ideation Stage

The decision to leave the ideation stage is a vote of confidence in your MVP; you are signing off on the concepts and tactics that you'll execute in the next stage. You'll know that you are ready to leave the ideation stage when you have evaluated the problem fully, explored its possible solutions and selected for testing the solutions that you believe will be most effective.

At this point, you might have more questions than you did when you started the Ideation Stage. That can be a good thing, as long as the questions you have center around a common theme: "How will we know if our MVP works?"

This, of course, is the whole point of ideation: To come up with a solution that will solve the problem. To understand whether your ideas will serve this purpose, you must be able to answer your question in data-driven form: "How will we *measure* how close we get to attaining success?" This must be addressed before you leave the ideation stage. What do you hope to accomplish with your MVP, and how will you measure it?

Answering the Big Question

When you picked your MVP, it's likely that you chose it because you needed to improve your organization's performance in some specific area of business. You might have felt a need for more leads, or for a larger number of followers on social media, or for any number of other things. So, to leave the ideation stage, you should return to your initial line of thinking. The answer to the big question—**"How will we know this works?"**—should naturally account for the metrics that were used to generate your MVP in the first place. In other words, to take the examples above, you'll know if your MVP works if you get more leads or more followers from its execution.

But that might not be enough. If your initial problem is measured by a lag indicator (like the number of leads that your marketing generates), you might have to measure other data that supports success. In other words, you may need to measure your MVP using lead indicators, in addition to the lag indicators you'll look at to show results.

This might not be simple to set up, because lead indicators and lag indicators aren't always as closely correlated as we'd like them to be. For example, how many sales calls would it take you to close one sale? If you've spent any time in sales, you know that the number of calls you make is correlated to the number of sales you close—but the calls don't *directly* cause sales. One month you may make 20 introductory calls and close 10 sales; the next month, you may make 30 calls and close three. When you perform the same activities and generate different results, you experience the gap between correlation and causation. Leading indicators are often *correlated* with success (in our example, calls are positively correlated to sales), but they're rarely tightly woven enough to create certain outcomes.

In order to know if your MVP works, you'll need to identify if the lead indicators you're using to measure its performance actually influence the lag indicators you're using to determine success. In other words, the MVP is the experiment you run to determine how close certain leading indicators are to causation.

So, using SMART goals, define the objectives of the MVP as lead indicators that your activity will strive to hit. You will use these measurements to evaluate the effectiveness of your activity in the cycle ahead. At this point, you'll run into one more issue: If you haven't done this type of activity before, how will you create realistic objectives around the lead indicators' outcomes? The answer is that you'll use benchmark data.

Benchmarks, Averages and other Sources of Contentment

The reality is that you only have a few possible options to shape objective measures of success for your MVP: You must use historical, proprietary and/or industry benchmarks.

HISTORICAL BENCHMARKS

Historical benchmarks are driven by data you've collected previously. These benchmarks are arguably the best place to start as you create objectives because they tend to account for more of the factors that are unique to your context. You might aim, for example, to improve results of your activity by 10% based on the returns you generated the last time. By using historical benchmarks, you can measure your own improvement. And you'll likely have some ideas as to how to improve, because if you're using historical benchmarks, you have probably validated that your MVP's lead indicators truly drive results. It's unlikely—although not out of the question—that you'd repeat an unsuccessful activity.

The drawback of using historical data is that sometimes it keeps your vision narrow and your expectations boxed into known outcomes. Using familiar benchmarks could limit your team's success in the Execution Stage by biasing them toward activities that only move the needle slightly and keeping them away from out-of-the-box actions that could yield huge results. Sometimes, it's worth remembering the saying: "What got us here, won't get us there." Keep your wits about you and your head up. If you myopically focus on historical data, you may not realize that the path you have taken is simply a dead end.

The second type of benchmarks are those that are based on third-party sources—usually providers of the marketing software your team uses—to set "industry averages." MailChimp, for example, provides "average email open rate" and similar studies. Buffer (a social media tool) provides "average post engagement" data. These sorts of proprietary benchmarks can be helpful if they are relevant to your situation and if they're viewed in the proper context. They do, though, have some limiting drawbacks.

The main issue with proprietary data is that it's often less relevant to your organization than your own historical data would be. For example, benchmarks for email statistics (like open rates and click-through rates) are widely available for a variety of different industries. Just about every email marketing tool has a "study" of benchmark data, and they'll often pull these studies automatically inside your campaign reporting to show you how you're doing compared to industry averages.

This information can be helpful, but the picture is blurred, and here's why: While the data *is* organized into industries, it typically doesn't account for a range of critical factors. The "average open rate in your industry" stat you see typically doesn't factor in how often other companies send emails, or what their subject lines say, or how big their lists are. Without those contextual clues, the benchmark is almost irrelevant to your organization and to measuring the success of your MVP. You need to see a context closer to your own business to set a better benchmark.

So, while third-party data can be helpful, you should use it to clarify a range of expected results but not to set a specific expectation for return. Proprietary benchmarks can set unrealistic expectations in both directions: Either you'll perceive that you've underperformed when you haven't, or you'll generate a false sense of success when you exceed "average" results that, in reality, were too conservative based on your context. When you set specific objectives for your MVP, only use proprietary data as a last resort.

INDUSTRY BENCHMARKS

The last and most valuable type of benchmark is an industry benchmark. These datasets are collected from companies just like yours via surveys. Companies like Profitcents and Sageworks focus on collecting this data on a volunteer or membership basis. In some industries, professional organizations or associations take on the task of collecting and sharing performance benchmarks with the industry. These benchmarks are useful because they are relatively affordable, specifically focused on companies

EXECUTING WITHOUT IDEATING IS LIKE GROCERY SHOPPING WITHOUT A LIST. YOU'LL HAVE SOMETHING TO SHOW FOR IT, ALL RIGHT—

BUT IT PROBABLY
WON'T BE THE
OUTCOME YOU
WANT, AND YOU'LL
PROBABLY SPEND TOO
MUCH ON THINGS
YOU DON'T NEED.

similar to yours and helpful in multiple areas of your business, not just in marketing.

These benchmarks also have their pros and cons. Their upside is that the data they use is collected on a volunteer basis from companies just like yours, so it's typically applicable to your context and far more targeted than the data that third-party software vendors provide. At the same time, despite the industry relevance of these benchmarks, they may not account for the specifics of your MVP and goals. That said, industry data tends to be both helpful and cost-efficient. You'll do well to consider it as you shape your objectives.

Moving On

You've put in the hard work of ideation. You've created your MVP and you know how you'll track its success. Now you're ready to see the results. It's time to execute!

Stage: Execution

THE EXECUTION STAGE

The goal of the execution stage is to act on the ideas compiled in your MVP and capture the results as data for assessment.

How This Stage Interacts with the Ideation Stage

The execution stage flows from and serves the ideation stage. As you've seen, the activity being executed is the brainchild of the ideation stage. Without proper ideation, execution would lack alignment; you would have no defined target for your activity and no way to measure its success. In other words, you'd have no way to tell the difference between activity and progress. As I'm sure you've seen, it's possible to have a lot of activity without creating any progress toward a goal. The ideation stage aligns activities toward your goal, so that in the execution stage, you can simply focus on tactical excellence.

Executing without ideating is like grocery shopping without a list. You'll have something to show for it, all right—but it probably won't be the outcome you want, and you'll probably spend too much on things you don't need.

So, not ideating at all is one problem. A communication gap between ideation and execution is another. To continue our grocery list analogy, it's easy to come home with the right food if you make the list. If someone else makes it, sometimes information is missing—you might come home with 2% milk when your spouse wanted skim.

Communication problems happen most often in bigger organizations or between distributed teams—scenarios where the team leading the Execution Stage is not the same team that created the MVP. This can lead to missing information on both sides. Sometimes the team that's executing is missing information that was assumed in ideation. On the flip side, sometimes what seemed like great ideas during ideation were not tempered by the realities of execution.

For example, let's say that the ideation team generated a goal to grow traffic on the website from 1k visitors to 5k visitors in one month using SEO without a paid media budget. This is a highly unrealistic goal; it doesn't account for the fact that SEO tactics take months to create results. The team responsible for executing could have informed the ideation team that paid media channels should have been part of the MVP—now, they're stuck executing with tactics that will almost certainly fail.

Mistakes like this can be dangerous and costly. If you can, avoid fools' errands by having a cohesive team responsible for all aspects of the cycle. If you can't—if your organization is too large or if team responsibilities don't allow for it—make sure that there is interaction and communication between groups in each stage.

How This Stage Interacts with the Assessment Stage

The Execution Stage is exciting. It will generate results and outcomes that will move the organization forward. Yet, while it's responsible for action, it's also responsible for creating data to be used in the next iteration of the cycle so that you can continue to progress.

The key to making this happen successfully is simple: **Measure everything.** At worst, you'll create a swath of data that has little relevance to your mission. On the other hand, if you assume that some data will be irrelevant and don't bother to capture it, you run the risk of shooting yourself in the foot—it could turn out that it was crucial in understanding your results.

Measuring everything makes even more sense when you consider that, once set up, the collection of data is a low-cost or no-cost endeavor for most organizations. Remember, once the execution stage is complete, you'll assess all of the data and outcomes to develop the most valuable assets produced by the process: insights.

Any and all questions your team answers in execution—even beyond the lead indicators that the MVP is focused on—may provide greater insight that will drive better results next time.

Budget and Time

How Much Time Do You Give the MVP?

The cost of most MVPs is tied to staffing and/or labor costs, which begs the question: How much time should your team allot to executing your MVP? There are two things to consider here.

FOCUSING ON THE MVP

Some things just take time. Ideally, budget should account for the time it will take to reach the goal you've set, not be arbitrarily fixed at some pre-determined line. Time estimates might have come up in the Ideation Stage, but if the team responsible for execution isn't the same one that ideated, they might have a different view on how long it will take to accomplish the goal. The importance of involving teams in all phases of the cycle can't be overstated. If everyone involved in the cycle is truly focused on reaching the goal, then multiple perspectives on the MVP should be heard throughout the process. Honest and open discussion will produce a more realistic expectation of what budget and effort will be needed to hit the goal.

ERR ON THE SHORT SIDE

If there is a range of expectations that results from budget discussions, err on the side of a shorter time frame. The reasoning doesn't stem from penny pinching, but from human nature: When people are asked how long they'll need to complete a task, most overestimate. (Interestingly, people tend to underestimate the amount of time that the same activity will take for someone else.) The team that is tasked with execution will likely fall into the fallacy of overestimation, and your job as the leader is to simply trim estimates for time toward a zone that incentivizes efficiency without putting adverse pressure on the project.

Another consideration is that, if you conservatively estimate time required for internal projects, you usually have the liberty to add more if it turns out to be needed. On the other hand, if you overestimate the time needed and provide your team close to the maximum amount from the beginning, you will have no room to expand. That reality is compounded by the truth of Parkinson's Law, which states that work will expand to fill the time given. Ever do a term paper in college the night before? You waited until the last minute because you could. You allowed the task to take up all the available time allowed. Without a constraint on time and budget, your team will do the same thing. Extend the timeline too far, and you'll leave yourself no room to manage the process.

How Much Money Should You Spend?

To determine a dollar-based budget, you should review another set of factors. Chief among them should be the measurement of return on investment, or ROI, in cold, hard cash.

In marketing, when you spend money on your MVP, you are usually buying something to impact a lead indicator. You might, for example, buy traffic by running pay-per-click ads, or buy assets to save production time for your team. As you spend, you should measure how much you get back.

This should come naturally. If you're embracing the "measure everything" mindset, you'll find it hard to move forward without knowing what you're getting in return for your money. You'll naturally want to know how efficiently you can increase clicks, impressions, engagements, etc. You'll also want to constantly compare costs to buy against the time your team or internal resource might spend.

For example, let's say you're creating a LinkedIn ad campaign and need to choose imagery. You could buy a $50 illustration and quickly put it to use to implement your MVP. Or you could have your team spend three to five hours to create a comparable illustration—which might incur double the cost and would slow down execution. In this scenario, buying the asset would positively impact your MVP's ROI by lowering your cost.

You may be able to sleep better at night if you "know" the dollar-based ROI of your activities, but theoretical knowledge shouldn't be confused with results. Put another way: Sometimes potential ROI doesn't translate to realized ROI.

Potential ROI involves using benchmark data to estimate what the returns on your investments might be in best-case, worst-case and average-case scenarios. Potential ROI is sometimes framed in the Ideation Stage, but realized ROI can't happen until the Execution Stage, where it's revealed as the dollars are spent. And sometimes ideation doesn't generate potential ROI at all. For example, there might be a directive in the MVP to "drive pay-per-click traffic to the website to create one lead." This directive doesn't account for how much the traffic might cost or how much one lead is worth, and that can be okay. Budget is generally defined in the Execution Stage because it can be difficult to frame realistically during ideation. Ideation is theory; ROI is the reality.

Be open to discovering what your budget should be as you execute. Consider the realities of the channels you're using. And certainly allow the execution team to contribute to your expectations. A willingness to

The MVP is the concept— the picture on the front of the puzzle box.

The work plan is the process—it tells you to start with the corners.

adapt can help you to move your lead indicators in the right direction.

Work Planning

Moving from an idea to a result takes real work.

The Ideation Stage created the MVP to give direction to the Execution Stage. The Execution Stage will use this direction to generate data and results.

Ideas are easy. They don't face the resistance of the real world. They can be blissfully unaffected by competition and people issues. When we have ideas, we rarely consider all of the difficulties involved in executing them. When execution gets underway and we begin to understand the realities of our budgets and the difficulties of the work itself, we're often surprised.

To increase clarity, the MVP needs to be translated into a work plan. The work plan will detail the activity that needs to be accomplished to reach the MVP's goal. It will break ideas into detailed, actionable steps that are assigned to people or teams. It will use project management to grow your seedbed of ideas into the fruit of tactical execution. It will turn dreams into action.

Some work plans might flow very clearly from the MVP. Others will require a bit of construction. They should be based on the desired results of the MVP, but they will require insight from the execution team to build out.

The MVP is the concept—the picture on the front of the puzzle box. The work plan is the process—it tells you to start with the corners.

Creating the Work Plan

You have to create a work plan to execute on the MVP because the work plan is what will transfer the intent of the MVP into explicit results. If the MVP is created correctly, its desired outcome will be clear. This allows the team that's executing to rapidly assemble the tactics needed to hit the goal and to use existing knowledge to execute with excellence.

This is where your team's knowledge and fervor come in.

START WITH WHAT YOU KNOW

One of the best ways to accomplish a goal is to start with the tactics you already have in place—or with those that you're familiar with and expect to work. This seems like a no-brainer, but using an approach that's already familiar to you (a "known entity") allows you to act with a reasonably predictable outcome.

For example, if you are trying to drive traffic to your website and you have just a few hundred dollars in budget, you might already know that buying content ads could drive the traffic you need under your constraints. It's simple to develop a work plan using tactics you already know. Ideally, known tactics should make up about 80% of your work plan.

You might also choose to use a known tactic with the belief that, based on new insight, you'll be able to vastly improve the results it generates this time around. This approach can work, but you should use caution when staking your hopes of success on it. In other words, don't rely on assumptions. Create your work plan with a deep respect for historical metrics. Be realistic about the activity and tactics you'll need to achieve your goals, even if you think there are reasons for optimism.

EXPERIMENT WITH THE UNKNOWN

As you create your work plan, you should also incorporate some tactics that you are not familiar with (or that you have no existing results with). This is the (scary) fun part of the whole process!

New tactics are the most difficult to manage and execute. They will take the majority of your management and focus, because executing them will be a learning endeavor in itself. Yet first-time tactics should only be allowed to make up 20% of your overall work plan. If more than 20% of the tactics in your work plan are first-time tactics, you're going to have a stressful execution stage because you'll have a far greater degree of uncertainty about whether or not you'll hit your goals.

When you add a new tactic to your work plan, you should rely on one of two assumptions: 1) you assume low expectations for the success of the tactic because you are completely new to its execution, or 2) you assume standard results from the tactic because you are using expertise or knowledge from an outside source.

If you're relying on the first assumption, you should be humble. You likely won't be able to accurately predict results, so look to outside data for guidance, then estimate conservatively.

For example, if you are planning to use Twitter ads to drive traffic to your website for the first time, research industry benchmarks first. Use them to predict your results, giving yourself buffer by expecting that you'll only achieve 80% of the benchmarks.

When you're new to execution, you shouldn't set goals that require above-average tactical ability. You should only require moderate, consistent, predictable results. If you take this approach of humility, you'll be more likely to hit your goals. Expect to learn from the execution this time and grow into better results when you use the tactic again.

SEPTEMBER

TACTIC	WHO	BUDGET		GOAL
Posting on Social Media 3x Per week	Jenny	$	800.00	1.2K Impressions, 400 Likes/Comments
CRO Edits to the Website	Kathryn	$	1,500.00	Increse time-on-page by .5 seconds
Monthly Email Campaign to Segment A	Jacob	$	850.00	Grow engagement by 4%
Monthly Email Campaign to Segment B	Lucy	$	850.00	Grow engagement by 3%
Pay-Per-Click Ads on Search Engines	Rhys	$	5,000.00	New Tactic, Discover Return Metrics
Conduct Webinar on Cyber Insurance	Elisabeth	$	15,000.00	Gain 200 new contacts

If you're relying on the second assumption, you should take a similar approach, but you can balance your expectations with the third party's historical results. When you outsource the management and execution of a tactic, you are benefiting from both the capabilities and the data of the third party. In other words, you should have a better means of estimating results and better means of achieving them. This can be a win-win for your organization.

With the known tactics and "first time" tactics in place, you have developed your work plan.

Effective Project Management

With the work plan in place, it's time to execute.

Now, this isn't a book on project management. There are already plenty of those; you can pick the flavor you like best and apply it to this process. But here are three principles that should influence how you manage execution:

1. Create a cadence of accountability.

You should have weekly meetings or checkpoints with your execution team to monitor progress toward your goals. Don't just wait around until the end of the cycle to find out if you'll hit the goals. Take the lead and meet regularly to evaluate the tactic's execution. This way, you can make sure that you're heading in the right direction. You will also use these meetings to capture and discuss data points.

2. Get people what they need.

If you find that a tactic is not generating the results you need, you may realize that your internal team needs training. This is a great way to identify areas for growth and then train up specific competencies. Your team might also need other resources, like books or guides, to help them on the journey.

3. Keep the goal in front.

Keep your conversations at the goal level. Don't get lost in the weeds of discussing exactly what your team members are doing to execute the tactic. This micromanaging causes two issues: First, it shows a lack of confidence in their ability, which can be deflating and can drive results down. Second, it takes ownership away from them, which puts it back on you. When the results don't happen, they'll blame your guidance, not their own ability.

Defining the End of the Execution stage

Before you jump into the Execution Stage, the last thing you need to define is when the phase will end. You don't want to let experiments run for too long without iterating on them, but you also don't want to cut things off just before they generate valuable insight. So, what is the best plan?

The best timeframes are based on weekly or monthly increments, not on arbitrary intervals (like every 8 days or something similarly absurd). You might specify a two-week or a one-month Execution Stage. The key is that your cadence should flow with the rhythms of your culture and workplace.

Here are two considerations on choosing your timeframe:

1. How long will the work take in the MVP?

If you are building a piece of software, you might need three to six weeks to even get the initial piece of code developed and deployed into a testing environment for people to use. So you could easily look at longer cycles. If you're running a pay-per-click ad campaign, on the other hand, you could be doing two- to three-day cycles. The nature of the work has a big impact on how long you should let a cycle run. Use common sense.

2. How much time will it take to organize?

Another consideration in setting a timeframe is how long it will take to organize and manage the work. If you are planning an Execution Stage with 40 people and 500 hours of work, it might take just a few weeks to plan the work, but it will probably make sense to run the work over a longer period.

Yet, here is the reality: As you become comfortable with the cycle process, you'll start to realize that you can move through your cycles as quickly or slowly as you want to. Your only limitations are yourself and the team around you. This is the real power of the model: You can be as reactive as you need to be. You can assess and ideate and execute on daily or even hourly cycles if it makes sense.

But to keep yourself and your team sane, you should begin more gradually. You'll soon learn the ropes of riding the tornado.

Common Factors of Successful Execution

At this point, it makes sense to break down the factors that impact the success of your execution. Use this brief guide as a simple diagnostic to figure out where your problems might be if you aren't achieving the results you expect.

The factors listed here are presented in order of decreasing frequency—people tend to be the most common cause of issues, followed by tools and then by tactics. As you root out issues, begin your diagnostics accordingly.

a. **Knowledge**. Do your people have the right knowledge to complete the task? Were they able to perform at or near industry benchmarks? Do they lack a critical understanding of the industry that caused a missed opportunity?

b. **Skills.** Are they matched up with the right types of tactics? Do they have the right skillset? They might be eager, but can they perform the task at a high level?

c. **Time.** Were they given the right amount of time to execute the tactic successfully? Were they bogged down in other work? Was the task too much for the given cycle?

TOOLS

a. **Capabilities.** Are you using the right tools for the tasks at hand? Did you spend more time doing manual tasks when things should have been automated? Where could tools or software have helped the process to run more smoothly or generate greater results?

b **Cost.** Are we using tools that have more capabilities than we need to pay for? Is our ROI impacted by these tools?

a. **Benchmarks.** How did we perform against the benchmarks for the tactic? Why did we get the results we achieved? Why did we excel or fail?

b. **Competition.** How did competition factor into the tactic? Were they stronger than before? Did we find a real competitive advantage in the market?

c. **ROI.** Did we achieve the results at the cost that we had hoped to?

Leaving the Execution Stage

With the Execution Stage complete, you're ready to move into the next phase of the cycle: the Assessment Stage. Yet before you leave this stage—both mentally and physically—you'll want to complete the following actions because they will become harder to accomplish once you move forward.

Feedback Loop and Data

You've now collected a lot of data from your activities, and you've likely realized that there is some data you didn't collect but should have. Take the time now to document what data you'd like to gather during the next cycle that could impact your work plan and execution in the future. Having good data can improve every part of the cycle, so take every opportunity to collect better data as you move along on your journey.

Also, you have surely found some areas where automation or better tools could have created better results. Make note of these areas, as well. All of these ideas should feed into your Assessment Stage, helping to build better execution in the next cycle.

Define the Dataset

Finally, as you wrap up execution, you'll want to document your MVP's dataset so that you can properly assess your activity and judge your results in the next phase. If you are not doing this personally, you should make sure that your team only uses the data associated with your MVP, not data from activities that are unrelated to the current cycle.

For example, if you were sending specific emails to your customer base as part of your campaign, but also sent a few newsletters to the same list during the same time period, you would not want to commingle the data from both activities. If you're having someone compile a report, make sure that they know this. Clarify the data you'll bring forward.

CONCLUSION

Now you have seen the three stages of the RTX Framework. You've seen how each stage interacts with the other two. And you've seen how following this cycle allows you to iteratively achieve your marketing goals.

Yet you've also probably formed some questions as to what this looks like in implementation—and how it might apply to *your* business, specifically. We can't dive into all the nuances of application for every business, of course. But in the final section of this book, we'll examine a few examples that will help you to see how this framework might be applied to your own marketing activities.

Let's give you a better lens into what the cycle looks like in a business's daily operations.

IMPLEMENTATION TOOLS & CASE STUDIES

This section of the book is aimed at helping you make the framework operational in your business. This means we need to turn the ideas and concepts we've discussed into some real-life tools and processes that you can act on.

But before we jump in, know this truth: This is not a one-size-fits-all implementation plan. These are examples that will likely work best for small teams (say, eight to 15 people) fit within a monthly cycle. You will need to consider if the applications here are right for your team, and what you might need to do to adjust them to your needs.

The best outcome is that you take the ideas and concepts presented here and use them to create tools that are tailored to your team and business.

Carry on.

STEP 1: ESTABLISHING YOUR GOAL

To begin the process, first establish your goal. Without a goal, this entire exercise can be a big waste of energy, resources and time. A strong goal is your antidote against waste.

SMART Goal.

For our implementation examples, we are going to follow the simplest and most approachable method of goal setting: the SMART goal method. SMART is an acronym that stands for Specific, Measurable, Attainable, Realistic and Timely. (See Appendix A for more details.)

To be effective, the goal you create has to have these simple attributes. One of the biggest reasons we don't achieve our goals is that we haven't articulated them well. For example, we may set a goal to lose weight. But if we fail to prescribe a specific number (say, 10 pounds), and if we fail to give it a time constraint (say, by the end of March), and if we don't plan for action (say, by avoiding fast food and exercising three times a week), we will never achieve our goal—and we'd have a hard time knowing if we had.

A productive goal will naturally answer the question, "When will I know I've reached the goal?" If you can't answer that question, your goal is not a SMART goal.

Once you've defined your marketing goal, you'll want to put it at the center of the process. It should be visibly displayed in the middle of your wheel to define the focus of your activities.

OWNING THE GOAL

As the team leader, you are responsible for establishing the goal. This means that *you* own the goal. If your inclination is to pass the goals down to your subordinates and give them ownership, you will run into one big challenge: *You* have established the goal. Your ownership of the goal represents your stake in the team and the outcome. The leader who tells his team to advance only to stay on the backline and disengage will probably not be a leader for very long.

You must own the goal. But you can create sub-goals for your team to share ownership of the plan you are working toward in the cycle. Sub-goals typically translate into lead indicators that your team can own and work toward to contribute to the main goal.

Your team should translate big goals (lag indicators) into sub-goal actions (lead indicators) and then take responsibility for those. You own the big goal, and your team can own sub-goals.

Communicating the Goal

Your well-defined goal becomes the center of your activities and the core of your mission. This needs to be communicated regularly with your team. Display the goal at the top of the scorecard that you'll create in the following section. The scorecard will serve as the center for communication and progress tracking with your team. Your sub-goals should be tracked on the scorecard or in another document that is displayed at each check-in. Be sure to note who is responsible for each.

You should communicate the goal and review your progress toward it every time the cycle moves forward. This will keep you aligned toward what you are aiming to achieve and remind the team of your progress. You might be surprised at how quickly busyness and distractions can sidetrack progress toward your goals. Keeping the goal in front of your team can have a big impact on your success.

With your goal in place and well communicated, you are ready to jump into your first cycle. It's time to begin the journey toward the results you want.

ASSESS

STEP 2: THE ASSESSMENT SESSION

First, a caveat: The RTX Framework ideally starts with the assessment stage, but that is not always possible, as you may be in the midst of a campaign when you commit to making this shift in your marketing process.

If you can bring ongoing activities to a close before beginning the cycle with assessment, that's advisable, but if you can't, then wait until your Execution Stage ends before you enter the Assessment Stage.

The Assessment Stage begins with a kickoff session—during which you review the current data, talk with the team and develop a mindset using your current set of insights. This meeting prepares the team to make the right decisions before you move into the Ideation Stage.

Pre-Work

The assessment session is unique in that you might have some personal preparation to do before you pull the whole team into the discussion. You'll need to locate, confirm and organize data in a way that's easy to understand so that in the meeting insight will come more easily. Many of the data points you're looking for may be part of your scorecard (see below), but for now, your job is to collect all the data you find valuable to the discussion of your goal.

As you select a goal, you'll often find many simple data points laying on the surface of the issue that seemingly point to the source of the problem and a readily quick fix. It may be too easy to use these readily available data points to build your claim of causality between those data points and your current state and rush into a solution. Your job is to dig deeper, underneath the assumptions, and look into all of the data around the problem that gave birth to the goal before you act. Don't rush it.

One artifact that you and your team must create in this process is a collection of data points that will help you track your progress toward your goal. This will be your scorecard. If you are just starting the process, you won't have an existing scorecard. That's okay; the data you collect as part of your assessment preparation might form the basis of your scorecard as you move forward.

Who: The Meeting Roster

The entire team should be in the Assessment Stage meeting. Everyone who has been or will be involved in the activities will have a perspective to share on the data that exists. Having multiple perspectives can lead to valuable insight into activities, guide interpretation of data and add confidence to your next steps as a team. As you get started with this process, err on the side of including participants—at least for the first few meetings until you see who adds value to the process.

What: The Agenda

1. Review the scorecard (or just data the first time)
What was on track? What was off-track?
Why did that happen?
What issues do we see?
How does this compare to benchmarks?
Do we have the right data?

2. Review the work
What were successful/unsuccessful tactics in moving the metrics?

3. Review the team
Did we have the right time devoted to the tasks?
Did we lack capacity or knowledge in the execution?

4. What did we learn?
What insights are we taking away from this cycle?
How do our insights impact the next cycle?

5. Conclusion: Insight

Record of insight to be delivered/reviewed at the next Ideation Stage.

Where and When: The Setting

You can hold this meeting anywhere you'd like. But it's important that you have access to your data and are able to ask questions with some level of privacy to allow for open discussion. When you start asking questions or reviewing a tactic, you might find that you need more data points. Or you might find that one person on the team underperformed. (They would probably appreciate this conversation not being shared with the waitress at your local restaurant.) Conducting this meeting internally makes sense. If you're already riding the tornado, have the meeting as close to the end of the execution cycle as possible, so that you can retain the freshness of activities and impressions during your discussion.

Outcome: The Go/No-Go Decisions

At this stage, you've gathered all the information you have available and you are left to make one critical decision: You and your team must decide whether you will move forward with a cycle or stop and reevaluate your goals.

In most cases, you'll simply spin up another cycle and continue to try to reach your goals. In other cases, you might make more substantial changes based on your assessment.

For example, you might change your tactics, or at least recommend different tactics based on your assessment. You might uncover insight that will change your team during the next cycle. Don't be afraid to propose new experiments or make tough decisions based on the insight you've uncovered.

Most organizations know already that many of the challenges preventing them from reaching their goals are related to people. These might be staffing issues (i.e., employees need more bandwidth) or capability issues (i.e., employees don't have the ability to get a job done). Acting on capability challenges can be tough. You might know that one of your team members is the cause behind the lack of results but fear firing them. The assessment stage is blind to personal preferences and emotions. It looks at data and presents that data as insight in the best way possible for leaders to make decisions. You'll have to take ownership to make decisions in your organization based on the insight this stage provides you.

Easier decisions are related to the tools and processes that are part of the approach. Review your data and see if you need to make a go/no-go decision on a tool or process, as well. Maybe this is the time to decide the new software was not worth it, or that you need software to do this more effectively. Seeing more clearly the challenges you have and what needs to happen to overcome them is the insight you now have in completing the cycle.

The End of the Assessment Stage

Ending the assessment stage should help you understand where you are in the process of reaching your goals, as well as the situational awareness you need to lead into the next stage of progress toward the goal. With this assessment session behind you, your team is armed with new insights and data that will influence the decisions you make in the next cycle. This is when you know the assessment stage is successful: When you have a greater sense of awareness and progress toward your goal and a clearer sense of what needs to change to reach that goal in the next cycle. The worst scenario is that you don't feel any closer to the right outcome. If that is the case, you missed something along the way in the assessment stage.

IDEATION

Step 3: Your First Ideation Session

The session is focused on generating ideas and possible actions around your marketing challenges. A simple agenda can keep the conversation focused and help to "herd cats" as the overall discussion might lead into important and otherwise uncovered issues in the people, process and approach to the goal process. Let your meeting flow, even to the point that it gets a bit off the rails at times, at least when you feel that tangents are productive or will contribute to the overall success of the project. But pull back to the agenda when you sense the discussion moves to items that do not apply to reaching your goal.

Pre-Work

When you create the list of attendees (see below), be sure to send expectations and an agenda ahead of time so that they can consider the goals and develop a frame of reference. Since they know this is a brainstorming session, they might have some ideas already, or they might take this time before the meeting to come up with some ideas to share. This can allow them some time to do the research

Case Study: Data Decisions

Takeaway: Using website analytics and search data to detect competitors in the market.

RKB is a leading chip board manufacturing company in the Mid-Atlantic region. They assemble chipboard components for different applications, from home appliances to aircraft, typically working on a contract production basis. Their commercial lines have ridden a steady stream of SEO leads to drive new business, but in recent months, the lead flow had died down. They had not changed activity, but their results had changed.

RKB had been enjoying the fruits of hard work in using the RTX Framework to reach a point where the lead generation from their marketing was predictable. Yet in seasons of abundance, we loosen our discipline and commitment to the process, and results can wane over time—this is what was happening to RKB.

When they returned to the disciplines of the cycle and committed to the Ideation Stage, they could see no real reason to change anything that had been working. Convinced that the results from the past where still there, they moved into execution and charted the results on the scorecard with the same decreasing results. The frustration and disillusionment were hard to watch as they seemed to feel blindsided by these falling results.

Then they went to the Assessment Stage but were still unable to get unstuck. Their previous success was blocking them from really looking into the data to see what was happening.

Our team pressed them to revisit the data and assisted them in the search to see what was going on. They were looking at their own scorecard without ever asking themselves what other data existed that might bring insight into the falling numbers.

We found two interesting pieces of data related to their organic and direct traffic that they had not been tracking: First, organic search rankings had been slowly falling over the previous six months for their core pages around certain products. Overall search traffic had dropped about 2%, so they had felt that their traffic numbers shouldn't be too big of an issue. But, on the services pages themselves, organic traffic had fallen 23%—something RKB hadn't realized. We found two competitors were now outranking RKB in search for these services. Now they had insight to work with.

Additionally, they had an 8% decrease in referral traffic, which was not seemingly correlated to new business. In digging deeper, they were right. It was not correlated to new business—but it was correlated to existing customer business. We shared with the account team data that two clients had decreased their orders and contracts by 4%, then 8% and now 20% over the previous quarters. When the account manager contacted the customer, they suspected that the customer was taking business elsewhere.

The failure to dig into the Assessment Stage can leave big holes in your insight on your sales and marketing efforts. Push deep until you find real insight. That is the core of this stage and can change the trajectory of your efforts and business.

and to come up with detailed rationales for the ideas they are thinking of. Busy people sometimes have a hard time coming up with ideas on the spot and appreciate the time ahead of the meeting.

Who: The Meeting Roster

The ideation session generates great ideas for achieving your goal. As Scripture states, "with the multitude of counselors, there is great wisdom," and you should follow suit on your own team. Invite everyone involved in the execution, for two reasons: First, it creates a sense of teamwork and opens communication that will be needed when the goals are not reached or tough conversations need to be had. This process thrives on having a great team that communicates well and believes in the same goal.

Second, and more important, great ideas come from many different perspectives. Including your entire team opens up the realm of possibilities of outcomes and pushes on convention. You remove tunnel vision and groupthink in a healthy organization and team that communicates well and has a safe environment to explore ideas.

The session itself requires two key roles: A facilitator who will lead the agenda and keep the conversation on course. This will likely be you. Additionally, you'll need a note taker or secretary. Ideas and thoughts will come up quickly and you'll need one dedicated resource to take notes. Choose a person who is a good note taker (ideally, someone whose note-taking won't inhibit them from contributing from the discussion). The same person should not be both the facilitator and the note taker.

What: The Agenda

1. Review the goal

What metrics are lead and lag indicators of this goal?

What actions support this goal?

2. Discuss any issues surrounding the goal achievement

What stands in our way of achieving this goal?

What don't we know?

What might need to happen to achieve this goal?

3. Discuss any current insights on the goal state

What data would be good to have that we don't?

Are we confident about the data?

What does this data mean?

4. Discuss the current tactics around achieving the goal

Are we doing the right things the right way?

Could it be a process problem or people problem?

Can we achieve more with better processes or tools?

5. Discuss the people and roles around achieving the goal state

Is it a process problem or person problem?

Are the roles aligned correctly?

6. Discuss solutions (building an MVP)

What could we do in the next 30 days to accomplish this goal?

What are we confident about or unconfident about?

What already exists to solve the problem?

What are the lead indicators we think match this goal?

How have others solved this goal?

7. *Recap ideas and work*

Work down to the best ideas that will focus your time and energy.

Store other ideas for later.

Where and When: The Setting

The best ideas come when we are free to think or stimulated to think differently. In his book *When*, Dan Pink notes that different types of thinking are ideally suited to different times of the day. If you are really trying to dig into data, hold the meeting in the morning. If you are trying to be more creative and off the wall, do it in the afternoon or at happy hour; just watch how happy it might get.

In the same vein, consider the location of the session. The same old conference room that every meeting is held in might not be the best bet. Maybe going on location to a place that is thematic to the problem, or doing the meeting outside, might be enough to change the mindsets of the participants to open up new ideas. Consider the time and the location as cat-alysts for the idea-generation process and important ingredients to the overall success.

Outcomes: MVP and Scorecard

Creating the MVP

As ideas are discussed and the conversation moves forward in your session, you will uncover both great ideas and a good bit of work that lies ahead. The note taker should capture the work and ideas so that you can make sense of it all at the recap.

The idea list will likely be the seed bed for your MVP for the coming execution cycle. Make a list of all the action items and tactics that come out of your meeting. This might be things like "start a PPC cam-paign" or "cold call 30 contacts a day." These are the raw material of your work plan for the Execution Stage.

Ideas that are generated sometimes need a bit more detail or research to move them into a validated state. After the ideation session, the work needed for those ideas could be created into tasks to be vetted in the work plan, or a short task list leading into the Execution Stage to figure out the final details.

For example, say the idea of "sending a video via an email" comes up in the meeting. That is a great idea, but no one knows how to do that, or even if it is possible. This would need to be researched and vetted before it becomes part of the work plan.

This process will naturally lead to more questions. There's no end to intellectual inquiry; it's simply halted by time and budget. Don't fret if you feel like you have more questions than when you started the session. This is the feeling of progress. Embrace the process, not the fact that you answered all your questions.

Defining the Scorecard

The second element that will arise during the session is the scorecard—the set of data points that will measure success. This is your catalog of lead metrics that you will track to reach your goals. This scorecard is the very pulse of data that will travel through all the stages of the cycle, providing context and measuring success.

In the ideation session you'll uncover logical lead and lag indications to your goal, and you'll want to start tracking them more aggressively to gain insight into the success of your organization and activities. Define the scorecard, including the data you have (or need to acquire) that you foresee impacting your progress toward the goal. As the team brainstorms marketing activities, also note the data you'll need in order to measure them.

Set a cadence for the data collection in your score-card that matches the length of your Execution Stage. For example, your scorecard might be updated weekly, if your cycle is a month long. Yet if your cycle is a week long, you might update the data daily.

With this data collection process, your team will get real feedback on how effectively the tactics are moving toward your goal.

EXECUTION
STEP 4: ORGANIZING THE WORK PLAN

In the Execution Stage, we take the baton from the ideation stage with the MVP and start to build a tactical work plan that will help us reach our goals. Some of the elements you might have great confidence in; some you might have very little. Regardless, the RTX Framework will help you achieve greater insight to build a sustainable model for marketing results and greater confidence in your goals.

Your work plan should focus on end results.

In this example, the activities are listed under the corresponding goal that they are focused on achieving. This gives the team the reminder of the goal they are trying to achieve while working the tactics and navigating the gap between actions and results. Additionally, the activities should have some expected outcome. For example, if you're aiming for a #1 ranking in Google for an SEO keyword, you'll want to put that as part of the expectations or measurement of success for that tactic. Execution will suffer when you don't communicate or manage the gap between expectations or goals and the tactics you are doing to achieve them. Your job as the leader is to keep the team focused on that gap.

Defining the Cycle Time

By this stage, you'll need to define the time you wish to invest in the activities. Will you work for three days before assessing results, or will you work a month? As a rule, 30 days should be the maximum time to capture data and develop insights on your actions.

Capturing Data

With the scorecard in place, you'll need to document the tasks required to capture the data you don't have. You might need to set up web analytics, or you want to use mouse tracking software. Use the work plan to get the right data metric set up early on in the cycle to bring that data into the Assessment Stage.

Case Study: Effectiveness of Facebook Advertising

Takeaway: Lack of ideation leads to mismanaged expectations, data and results.

Flam Co. is a medical device manufacturer and distributor in the U.S. They manage their own Facebook Ad campaigns with a budget of around $12K a month. They primarily distribute CPAP masks and accessories.

In the culture of the organization, ideas are not ideas, they are mandates. When the boss tells you to do Facebook ads, they'd better be running by the next day. In this case, the team was spending much of the budget promoting two CPAP machines they sell to an audience of typical users: males who are over 50 and overweight.

The results were nominal at best: Click-throughs were not converting to sales.

The core issue was a lack of ideation around the campaign itself. Per the company's "do what management says" culture, the marketing team acted quickly without considering the type of ads, the channel and product they should focus on. Their campaign was reactionary, with the biggest concern being job security, not sales. The marketing team had previously tried Facebook advertising with little result, yet they hesitated to counter management's directive to run the Facebook campaign. Caught between a rock and a hard place, so to speak, they recycled the same ads they had run before and saw similarly poor results.

The RTX Framework aided the FlamCo team by stopping the process and allowing the ideation stage to drive innovation and decision making, rather than allowing those things to be driven by a top-down mandate. They were able to bring the whole team together and start at the right place in the discussion, which is the goal, never the tactic. During the ideation session, the marketing manager explained, "The CEO does not see our products on Facebook and wants to see them there." The ah-ha moment hit everyone—they were executing before assessment and ideation.

With this revelation, the team could now easily see the error of not following a data-based approach for solving the marketing problem. They took a step back from the previous position and reviewed the data and insights they had on the market. The leader of the team brought additional insights to the team through interviews with customers (another great source of data), and presented the concept of selling the consumable aspects of the machines, such as the masks. With these insights the team realized they could be on Facebook, solving the CEO issue, and actually move product and create results. All of this came about through a shift in the focus of the activity and by following a data-based process.

They set up the Execution Stage with new ads, and, sure enough, the e-commerce store saw more conversions than ever before. Still, more work was needed; as the marketing team gained insight, they structured the campaign to focus on different products and expanded goals.

Additionally, the marketing leader was able to go back to the CEO and share the data from the Assessment Stage and insights to firm up her position and case for the marketing team. This led to a promotion and more marketing budget in future years.

Being Selective

Lastly, you'll realize that you have more ideas than budget or time to get them done. It will be up to you and the team to make the final determination on what tactics make it into the work plan. Budget and time are great constraints to help you prioritize your work plan, but other factors may come into play—such as available staffing or tools—that will weed out any impractical tactics.

STEP 5: DOING THE WORK

With the work plan fully vetted, organized and assigned, the work begins. This is an exciting time as the ideas are applied to the real world and data starts to be collected on the effectiveness of the tactics toward reaching your goals.

Weekly Check-ins

Set a cadence of check-ins with your team to review issues, challenges and the data around your overall work plan. Unforeseen issues may arise in the month of your work plan that cause you to rethink or shift your priorities. The weekly check-in serves as the time for realignment on the goals and progress review with the team.

Fight the Urge

If you set the work plan for a month, and two weeks into the plan you start to see the data curve in the wrong direction, you might be tempted to change the plan. If you've embraced this model, this urge is completely natural. The logic seems clear: If something is not working, let's change it.

The answer to this is a bit more complicated; it's a yes-and-no situation. Yes, in the sense that if you feel 100% confident that you are right in your assertion, then you should stop the activity. A better solution is to make changes to the tactic to see if you can bring it back on course.

SEPTEMBER

TACTIC	WHO	BUDGET	GOAL
Posting on Social Media 3x Per week	Jenny	$ 800.00	1.2K Impressions, 400 Likes/Comments
CRO Edits to the Website	Kathryn	$ 1,500.00	Increse time-on-page by .5. seconds
Monthly Email Campaign to Segment A	Jacob	$ 850.00	Grow engegement by 4%
Monthly Email Campaign to Segment B	Lucy	$ 850.00	Grow engegement by 3%
Pay-Per-Click Ads on Search Engines	Rhys	$ 5,000.00	New Tactic, Discover Return Metrics
Conduct Webinar on Cyber Insurance	Elisabeth	$ 15,000.00	Gain 200 new contacts

For example, if you are running Facebook Ads and you're not getting the clicks you want, change the ad instead of stopping the spend altogether. This will keep the tactic on the board to the end of the cycle, allowing you to gather more conclusive data about the performance of the channel (is Facebook the wrong platform?) vs. the tactic (is the ad messaging off-key?). This is where most companies fail in digital marketing. They execute, but poorly. It's as if they dumped a new puzzle on a table and they are surprised that they can't make out the picture.

On the "no" side of that argument in the example above, you should tweak the ad rather than ending the campaign early because you don't know what you don't know. Learning is part of the process, and you can't make a smart decision about a particular tactic when you abandon it midstream. Let it play out, learn, adjust.

Using the Scorecard

The scorecard in this phase of the cycle is focused on capturing data to allow your team to see the progress of the activity toward the goal. The data you already have built into your operations should be added immediately, and the data points that are collected as part of the work plan should be added as soon as they are available.

Reviewing this scorecard at the weekly check-ins will help your team keep the goal as the big picture and will allow the data to start to build the bridge over the gap between execution of activity and progress toward the goal.

Explore the data not only in the literal aspect of the data, but give more meaning and insight to how it correlates to results. For example, if you are tracking website hits and you are below the goal, you might explain how this metric has been a direct correlation to the overall success of the goals in the past. In other words, numbers by themselves tend to not mean anything. They need to be put into context of the goal and given meaning by the leader. This helps your team understand and gets buy-in on the overall tactics that you are asking them to do.

Keeping track of the data keeps everyone focused on the goal. It is very easy in these digital channel and tools to get wrapped up in the tool itself, the features and enhancements, getting distracted from the goal you are trying to achieve.

First Lap Complete

When you've finished the Execution Stage, you have just completed the first iteration of the RTX Framework and it's time to start over. Heading back into the assessment stage, you now have new data, new tactics and new information to share and unpack to help assess your goal progress.

Gather all of this information and schedule your assessment meeting with the team and prepare to gather data, publish insights and move closer to reaching your goal.

Case Study: Turning Vague Requirements into Actionable Work

Takeaway: How a big goal translates into work around a disconnected goal. How you go from "more leads" to something actionable in your work.

JAnderson Consulting needed to boost lead generation for their mobility consulting practice. They never really had a grip on how to generate leads; they seemed more serendipitous than scripted. They executed marketing, trying this and that, until they had social media messaging, email marketing and an expensive website that were not doing anything for their lead generation efforts.

They were never short of ideas or goals. When they implemented the RTX Framework, the goals and Ideation Stages came very easily to the team. The challenge set in as the marketing group struggled to turn those goals into a work plan that generate results.

We focused on all the ideas and tactics they generated in the Ideation Stage and started to drill down into the priorities of the work they put into the work plan.

When we asked what results their marketing generated, they were stumped. They had data but didn't know how to use it. This is the core challenge in setting priorities for JAnderson. They did not know what work equated to movement on the metrics that impacted to success.

For this we had to spend some time in an assessment of the last cycle of activity and revisit the Ideation Stage. We dug up the data and helped them develop the insight they needed to reframe the ideas they had about reaching their goals. With the insights in place, they were very quickly able to see that many of the activities had not produced results and could be eliminated. Additionally, they saw the need for more tactics to support the ones that were generating some results to push them over the edge into lead generation.

With this new ideation complete, they could prioritize the work plan focused on the goals with greater confidence in the Execution Stage. The planning paid off. They started to develop the funnel they had hoped and have gone on to develop multiple lead generation campaigns for the business lines. They embraced data and used that to influence the work that led them to results.

BEYOND
THE BOOK

You've done it. You've finished the book and hopefully you've learned and seen the results that the RTX Framework can have in your own organization and you are excited to take it from here.

Now I can let you in on my hidden agenda in the structure of this book.

In the same way that the cycle allows you to ideate, execute and assess your marketing, this book is structured to allow you to take the system and make it your own following the same framework.

The first section was designed to woo you into understanding why you had to take a different approach to your marketing and problem solving in the business climate we operate in.

The second section gives you the core ideas around the framework. These are the big pictures of what you need to be thinking about when you are ideating around how this process works in your organization and what you are trying to achieve. This was designed to implant the ideas that need to be the seed bed for your own thinking: The "whys" behind the three stages and how they go together.

The third section was an example of how you can execute the framework in your organization today. There are sample agendas and directions on how to complete your first cycle. Follow these the first time out and see the process through to the end of the first cycle.

And when you finish that, the next assessment stage is yours to own. What did you learn? What can your organization do better? What did you miss? Your assessment of the framework itself is your own and you can make the go/no-go decision on the whole concept or carry it forward now to see your work plans—in fact, your very approach to marketing—take off in your organization.

You've been empowered to make your organization a rapidly thinking and executing organization that is no longer buffeted by the winds of change. You have the tools in your hands, and your mission is just beginning. But I've moved you out on top, riding the tornado. Now own it!

GODS

PEED

APPENDIX A

GOALS

SMART Goals

Goals: How to Get the Most Out of Your Life, by Zig Ziglar (Book)

https://en.wikipedia.org/wiki/SMART_criteria

https://www.mindtools.com/pages/article/smart-goals.htm

https://blog.hubspot.com/marketing/smart-goal-examples

Other Resources:

Traction: Get a Grip on Your Business, By Gino Wickman (Book)

The 4 Disciplines of Execution: Achieving Your Wildly Important Goals (Book) by Chris McChesney, Stephen Covey, Jim Huling

https://agilemanifesto.org/

CPSIA information can be obtained
at www.ICGtesting.com
Printed in the USA
JSHW051539180121
10962JS00004B/10